Brainstorms and Lightning Bolts:
Thinking Skills for the 21st Century

David D. Thornburg, Ph.D.
dthornburg@aol.com
http://www.tcpd.org

Thornburg, David D.
Brainstorms and Lightning Bolts: Thinking Skills for the 21st Century

ISBN 0-942207-13-0 (pbk.)
Copyright © 1998 by David D. Thornburg and Starsong Publications

Published in the United States of America.

ISBN 0-942207-13-0

Dr. Thornburg can be contacted at:
Thornburg Center
P. O. Box 7168
San Carlos, CA 94070
415-508-0314
DThornburg@aol.com
http://www.tcpd.org

Dedication

It is an honor to dedicate this book to the memory of my father, D. Robert Thornburg. He was a constant source of inspiration to me, and he helped shape my inquisitiveness and channel it into productive enterprises. Any good I have done is a mere reflection through the facets of his life.

As someone who helped me develop my ability to separate what's what from what's not, I think he would have liked this book. Unfortunately, I didn't write it fast enough, so I'll never know. Even so, his spirit infused my mind and heart as I wrote each page.

Thanks, Dad — I miss you.

Contents

Introduction

I'm sitting in my San Francisco office during the end of our recent bout with El Niño — a period where California was hit with incredible amounts of rain as a result of a small increase in the temperature of the ocean current off the coast of Mexico. The global impact of this event has been tremendous — tornadoes left their scars along the Southeastern part of the country, a balmy Midwest winter turned viciously cold overnight, and, a few miles from my office, houses went sliding into the Pacific Ocean.

Transformations of this magnitude are not uncommon in nature. But that isn't the only place they are happening. Large established businesses are experiencing El Niños of their own. Companies whose future was once secure are now finding the landscape of their businesses in a state of flux. Furthermore, new competitors seem to spring up overnight. Many of these new ventures are starting in college dorm rooms, not within the labs of existing companies. Corporate size, once an asset, is now a liability for some firms as they struggle to adapt in the face of rapid change.

Add to this the emergence electronic commerce and global competition on an unprecedented scale, and you can see that the shape of business is changing in incredible ways.

Coupled with this rapid change is the need for our educational system to prepare students for life in a new century — a century in which the rules have changed markedly from the rules in place during my youth. High-tech skills, once a luxury, are now essential for the bulk of the well-paid workforce in our country. As of March, 1998, there were over 358,000 vacant jobs in the information technology sector — high-paying jobs that were going begging because there were not enough skilled people in the job market to fill them.

Technology aside, we have entered a world that is zipping into the future at light-speed — a world where new thinking skills are needed in order for people to thrive in the economy of the next century.

And that brings me to this book.

This book has a few functions. First, I hope it serves as a wake-up call to any who think that the future is going to be an extrapolation of the past. Second, it presents a framework for thinking intelligently about the future, based on our hypothesis that our model of time needs to change and, along with it, the manner in which we think and act in the world of education and business. Third, we'll present some concrete, practical tools you can master to help you navigate through these times of turbulence — tools for creativity, for model building, for inventing your own future.

While each of these tools has a paper-based form, they each can be facilitated through the use of software. Where appropriate, we'll explore some of the software tools that make sense.

What do I mean by "making sense"? Just that the tools we mention actually add value to the process rather than hinder it. In our race to embrace technology, we sometimes get carried away, using a $900 palmtop computer to jot down notes that would be as easily captured on a slip of paper. I've worked very hard to be sure that the software described adds value to the processes we'll explore. Yes, you'll be using your pencil and paper to learn these tools, but some of you will find the computer-based tools to be as indispensable as your word processor or e-mail system.

In crafting this book, I had to make some guesses about my audience. First, your interest in this topic suggests to me that you are likely to have access to a personal computer and to the World Wide Web. For this reason, you'll see Web sites referenced every so often. Second, my guess is that you are either a business person, an educator, or a parent who wants to be sure that your offspring will be able to thrive in the coming years.

You might find some of the content counter-intuitive — I certainly do not argue for continuation of the status quo. You may find yourself resisting some of my ideas. If so, this is great! If my ideas are hard to swallow, it is probably because they run counter to your prior experience (or that they are wrong). No matter which, my goal is to challenge your thinking in some interesting ways and to provide some tools that will be of great utility to you, no matter what.

Of course, I have tried to do my research carefully. Any errors that emerge are my personal responsibility, and I apologize in advance for any errors you may detect.

I want to thank those who helped by reading and commenting on early drafts of this manuscript. I have taken their suggestions to heart. In particular, I want to thank Norma Godoy, Ron Voth, Lynell Burmark, Sara Armstrong, my wife, Pamela Thornburg, and others named in the body of the book itself.

And, finally, I need to make a disclaimer. I mention some companies in this book that are doing some interesting things. I will be mentioning them purely to illustrate a point. I do NOT give investment advice. If you find a particular company interesting to you, please contact your broker for more information before investing. Also, all product names mentioned are trademarked by their owners. With few exceptions, I have chosen to eliminate clutter in the text by mentioning this fact here, rather than putting the marks on each name as it appears.

Well, the sun is making its appearance — perhaps for an hour, or a week. What a great time to start exploring the future!

David Thornburg
San Francisco, CA, May, 1998.

The Future
Isn't What It Used to Be

The future arrived, it just wasn't evenly distributed.
— *William Gibson*

People sometimes ask me what futurists do. While I can't speak for all my colleagues, I can tell you what I *don't* do — I don't forecast the future.

There are two reasons for this. First, the future is intrinsically unknowable in detail because it is shaped by "wild cards" — inventions or discoveries that haven't happened yet. For example, when the automobile was invented, suburbs as we know them were unheard of. At the dawn of aviation, the railroad companies thought their future was secure. The original microprocessors were designed for use in vending machines and other fixed-function devices. Once cars, planes and microprocessors were invented, we could start to think about their impact. It would have been impossible to anticipate the impact of these wild cards until they appeared. While I don't know what wild cards are on the horizon, I'm sure there are plenty of them, and that some of these will have a profound effect on our lives.

Second (and fortunately), I don't need to forecast the future — there are plenty of prototypes in research labs and corporate offices to keep me busy with the short term future. As these existing ideas make it to market, my colleagues and I have the pleasure of thinking about what their impact might be on education, work, and leisure. It is a lot easier (and safer) to explore emerging ideas than it is to gaze into a crystal ball and try to imagine life in the next millennium. This latter task is one I gladly leave to William Gibson, Bruce Sterling, Neal Stephenson, Arthur Clarke and other excellent authors of science fiction.

11

Sometimes, the impact of even successful inventions can be misunderstood by their inventors. One example of this was suggested to me by Professor Fred Litto at the Universidade de São Paulo (USP) — the story of Marconi and Bell.

Alexander Graham Bell is credited with the invention of the telephone in 1876. While his first demonstrations of the telephone were for transmitting voice, he felt that it was the ideal tool for people who wanted to listen to concerts and plays from the comfort of their homes.

Around 1897, the Italian inventor Guglielmo Marconi developed wireless telegraphy — radio. His invention allowed messages to be sent from point to point across the Atlantic. Even after moving his operations to the United States in the early 1900's, his view of radio was that it was an ideal tool to support point-to-point communication. When one of his New Jersey employees wrote a memo suggesting that radio could be "broadcast" to large audiences, his proposal was rejected. (This employee, David Sarnoff, went on to found RCA).

So here we have something truly interesting: Bell, the inventor of the telephone, thought he had invented radio. Marconi, inventor of radio, thought he had invented the telephone.

Hindsight, of course, is always perfect. But these examples serve to illustrate an important point. Even when you look at technologies that already exist, it is quite possible to completely miss the applications that will make them indispensable.

This caveat aside, let's explore a "future" technology that is already here. Let's look at speech recognition software. The ability of computers to recognize spoken words has been the quest of researchers for about three decades. While some progress has been made over the years, we are starting to see tremendous improvements in the past year or so. These improvements have come from two sources. First (and most importantly) the engineers and scientists working in this area are doing a stellar job. Second, the power of the computers sitting on our desks (or palms) today is orders of magnitude higher than what existed just a few years ago, allowing an incredible amount of computational horsepower to be purchased at an affordable price.

As a result, we have programs like *Naturally Speaking*, a speech recognition system for personal computers developed by Dragon Systems (http://www.dragonsystems.com).

How well does it work? Well how has this chapter looked so far? I dictated it to the computer and it was captured with about 90% accuracy.

Looking at this program, I ask myself a series of questions: What will it mean for the future of typing? What impact will this technology have on secretarial jobs? Will schools take advantage of this type of software? If they do, how can it be incorporated in a classroom with everyone talking at once? If computers of the future no longer need keyboards, what might they look like?

The reason these questions are worth exploring now is because speech recognition is getting good enough to be useful.

These speculations are fun to play with. In fact, you should create some answers to these questions yourself. Better yet, think about the kinds of questions *you'd* like answered regarding the impact of speech recognition technology. And, don't forget the lesson of Marconi and Bell — we might find speech recognition being used in ways we can't imagine today.

So, with this introduction to the futurist's task, I'll move to the meat of this chapter — my sense of some emerging trends that will be important in the coming years. Remember that I'm not looking in a crystal ball; everything I write about in this chapter has already happened somewhere.

First and foremost, the pace of change is accelerating. It is common to hear that the total volume of information on the planet is doubling every 18 to 24 months. This tidbit is tossed out as a quick one-liner, and most people who hear it don't stop to think about the implications of this statement. Let's look at this statement more carefully: Think about the sum total of all discoveries made since the beginning of time. Now imagine an equal number of new discoveries being made in the next 18 months. *That* is what this sentence is telling us.

Personally, I find this to be incredible — unbelievable, even. And yet, there is little argument with the idea that we are living in a time of amazingly rapid development in many areas. For example, in the 1980's it took nine years to find the gene for cystic fibrosis, yet in 1997 the gene for Parkinson's Disease was found in nine days. Scientists at the Monterey Bay Aquarium Research Institute (MBARI) are discovering new life forms weekly — all in an underwater canyon located a few miles off the coast of California. Even if the time for information doubling is wrong, it is pretty clear that we are living in a period of rapid discovery, invention and change.

The impact of rapid information growth would be tremendous if it existed all by itself. In fact, it has some help: the collapse of the "information float." The information float is the time lag between a discovery and its application. Moveable type was known for many years before it was applied to the mass production of books. The typewriter was a curiosity for many years, as were many inventions of the late 1800's. And yet, today, new discoveries are turned into products almost overnight. It is as if the marketing department was hanging out with the scientists and engineers every day looking for new ideas to turn into products. And, the public stands ready to purchase these products when they meet a need.

What does rapid change mean for organizations? What does it mean for companies large and small? What does it mean for educational institutions, ranging from Kindergarten through college?

Professor Ikujiro Nonaka at UC Berkeley has this to say on the topic: "The dynamics of knowledge have become the most important competitive resource of the firm."

Note what he is saying — it is the *dynamics* — the rate of change of the information, not the information itself, that is the important resource. We'll revisit this topic later in our chapter *From Nouns to Verbs*. For now, suffice it to say that we are living in a world of constant change, and business and education models based on steady-state views of the world will fail.

If there is one conclusion that can safely be drawn from this, it is that we need to rethink our model of time. Most of us grew up in a world that was fairly predictable. Many things stayed the same, or changed slowly. Those that changed rapidly, seemed to move in a linear fashion. When chaos struck (as it did in the 1929 stock crash) most people were ill-equipped to deal with the aftermath. Today's world is quite different. Change seems to have accelerated, and time is becoming increasingly non-linear. (For example, we hear a lot these days about "Internet years" — a modern version of "dog years" where one calendar year equals seven years in "Internet time").

The emergence of a new technology in the marketplace not only takes place almost overnight, but new ideas often grow exponentially. Consider this: From 1980 to 1990 the personal computer industry grew from zero to $100 billion dollars per year, making it the fastest growing industry in history. The rapid emergence and acceptance of new products and services is catching established corporations by surprise.

Changes of this magnitude were unknown in the relatively quiet years of the past. Old models of business and education were built around a linear concept of time. Bells and whistles regulated the flow of work and instruction. Efficiency was measured in terms of parts per hour. The clockwork universe seemed adequate to define our world. Corporate leaders referred (with straight faces) to "five-year plans."

In his book, *Real Time*, Regis McKenna draws a contrast between the business world prior to 1975, and the world since that time. Prior to 1975, innovations were developed by large institutions who then diffused them into the marketplace where the public was left to accept them. After 1975, innovations were increasingly created by new ventures who then took them to market where they were accepted by a public eager for new ideas. This left large established institutions in the position of reacting after the fact.

If the old world was defined by linear "clock" time, the new world is defined by chaos theory. The linear incremental world of the past no longer exists. In its place we have a world defined by non-linearity — by the world of chaotic behavior. New products emerge overnight. Established markets shift almost instantaneously.

The world of non-linear systems has been the subject of much research in the past twenty years, much of it focused on a branch of mathematics called "chaos theory." While the details of chaos theory are outside the scope of this book (several popular books on the topic, such as *Chaos — Making a New Science* by James Gleick will bring you up to speed), there are two aspects of this theory that have strong implications both for business and education. These aspects are:

1. The "butterfly effect," and,
2. Strange attractors

We'll explore the business and educational ramifications of these concepts in later chapters, but for now we'll get them defined for you.

The Butterfly Effect

The term "butterfly effect" has an interesting origin. It comes from the idea that a butterfly flapping its wings in Taiwan could cause a tropical storm off the coast of Florida. Whether this is factual is not the point — it is a graphic way to say that weather patterns are so sensitive to small fluctuations as to be intrinsically unpredictable over the long term.

Certainly this fits with common experience. How many times have you heard a glowing weather report for your area only to see the skies cloud over in a few hours, followed by a deluge shortly thereafter? Before you blame the meteorologists, you have to understand that the dynamics of weather patterns are extremely sensitive to initial conditions. The slightest inaccuracy in the starting data results in wildly divergent results down the line.

Why does this happen? Primarily because the weather (along with many other phenomena in the world around us) is controlled by non-linear processes — processes for which linear extrapolations of the current state do not apply, and for which small fluctuations at one end of the process can produce large changes later.

As it turns out, this chaotic behavior can be observed in very simple mathematical functions that are iterated over and over again. Just about any introductory book on chaos theory will provide you with some concrete examples to explore on your own, and a quick search of the World-Wide-Web will reveal many sites devoted to this topic.

For now, all we have to remember is that non-linear systems can produce chaotic behavior. These systems are found in nature, and they are found inside organizations of all kinds.

Strange Attractors

When many people first start exploring chaos, they equate it with randomness. This is a mistake. While it is true that the future state of a complex system (such as the weather) may not be predictable, neither is it random. The evolution of a system's behavior over time can take the form of a "strange attractor."

"Great," you might be thinking, "what's THAT?"

Well, first we need to define what an attractor is. Fortunately, that part is easy. Think about a simple pendulum — a rock tied to a string, for example. If you hold the string steady (or tie it to some place where the rock can hang free) and give the rock a push, it will swing back and forth, and (thanks to friction) ultimately stop at the bottom of the swing. This point is called the attractor, since it is the ultimate destination of the rock over time.

Many "well-behaved" mathematical functions have simple attractors like this: stable points to which the function settles down after a sufficient number of iterations.

Non-linear systems that exhibit chaotic behavior have different types of attractors. These systems seem to bounce around from place to place, with no predictable sequence, yet each state of the system fits into some overall pattern.

To give an example of a strange attractor from mathematics, let's try a little experiment. Start by placing three dots on a page to mark the corners of a triangle (shown as *A*, *B*, and *C* in the figure below). Next, pick a random location on the page (shown as *X* in the following figure). It doesn't matter where this point is — you just pick it at random.

Now, here is the task: Choose one of the three points *A*, *B*, or *C*, at random and make a dot *midway* between the location of *X* and whichever point (*A*, *B*, or *C*) you chose. This dot represents the new location of *X*. Now, just keep repeating this process, placing dots at each new location, and try to imagine what the resulting picture will look like.

A ●

X ●

C ●   *B* ●

When I've done this in workshops, many people think the resulting picture will just show a random array of dots. After all, the starting point was chosen at random, and the destination point is chosen at random (from among the three available) as well. Most folks are unprepared for the picture that results.

The resulting figure is called a Sierpinski gasket, after the mathematician who discovered it. This is an incredibly complex figure. At this level of magnification you can see that it consists of triangles nested within triangles. In fact, the nesting goes on to infinity.

This amazingly complex figure is the result of repeating the random corner selection process we described above. It does not matter what starting point we choose — we always get the same figure. This robustness of strange attractors is an important quality. Certain types of systems lock in to a specific behavior patterns, no matter how you choose the starting conditions.

While the topics of butterfly effects and strange attractors come from modern mathematics, they have analogs in organizations of all kinds. In this book, I'll refer to these terms in their capacity as metaphors. When I want to talk about systems that are very sensitive to initial conditions, I'll refer to the butterfly effect. When I talk about systems that seem to have a stranglehold on reality, I'll refer to strange attractors. I trust that you'll allow the metaphors to reflect the spirit of the concept, and not get overly concerned about the mathematics.

Now that we've defined our terms, you might want to explore your own organization for examples of butterfly effects and strange attractors. I've listed this as an activity for this chapter.

Activities for this chapter:

1. As these words are being written, January 1, 2001 looms on the near horizon. With the new century this close at hand, write your impressions of the skills, attributes and habits of mind that will be the mark of an "educated person" in the coming century. This activity should be done before reading further, and then compare your list with some of the ideas we'll be sharing later.

2. Think about your organization. What aspects of your profession seem to be driven by the linear model of time? What aspects seem to be driven by a chaotic model of time? (A worksheet for this activity is provided at the end of this book).

3. Using the appropriate worksheet at the back of this book, examine your organization or industry for examples of butterfly effects — areas where small, seemingly inconsequential events are producing tremendous changes. Then, look for strange attractors — behaviors or policies that appear locked in place, virtually impervious to change, even if they no longer meet any productive purpose.

From Incrementalism to Revolution

You can't cross a chasm in two jumps.
— Proverb

"Stick to the knitting." This sage advice was offered by management consultants Tom Peters and Bob Waterman in their best-selling book, *In Search of Excellence*. The idea, of course, is that companies should remain with the business they know best, and not diversify into remote areas where they lack expertise. This rule was one of eight that, in 1982, governed the operation of "America's best-run companies."

So, imagine our surprise when, short six years later, Tom Peters wrote *Thriving on Chaos: Handbook for a Management Revolution*. Suddenly, the world of business had catapulted into a period of incredible change and uncertainty. As Peters said in this book;

> There *are* no excellent companies. The old saw "If it ain't broke, don't fix it" needs revision. I propose: "If it ain't broke, you just haven't looked hard enough." Fix it anyway.

> No company is safe. IBM is declared dead in 1979, the best of the best in 1982, and dead again in 1986. People Express is the model "new look" firm, then flops twenty-four months later.

> In 1987, and for the foreseeable future, there is no such thing as a "solid," or even substantial lead over one's competitors. Too much is changing for anyone to be complacent.

In the previous chapter I mentioned the butterfly effect — the capacity of small events to produce huge consequences at a later time and place. In this book I'll refer to "butterflies" when talking about small changes that have huge consequences.

In today's environment of chaos, butterflies are emerging from their chrysalises at an incredible rate. Any organization that thinks it can "increment" its way to greatness and stability is on its way out of existence. Ventures need to be on the constant lookout for small shifts and developments that can have profound impact on their business.

Let's illustrate this with a concrete example.

In the early 1980's Sandra Lerner and Len Bosack were at Stanford University. She was in the business school, and he was on the staff of the computer science department. These lovebirds wanted to keep in touch during the day. Unfortunately, each department used a different network, and so they couldn't send e-mail to each other. The business school ran on an HP 3000 computer, while the engineering school ran on an HP 9000. Even though both of these computers were made by the same company, they could not interoperate within a network.

What was needed was a "router," a piece of equipment that would handle all the format translation and direct messages across network boundaries seamlessly. While telephone companies had to deal with similar problems on their networks, their equipment was much too expensive for small institutions to afford. So, Sandra and Len created an inexpensive router to meet their needs. The butterfly had been born!

Armed with the success of this prototype, Sandra, Len and three others decided to form a company around this product — Cisco Systems.

Cisco was founded in 1984. From the time it went public in April, 1990 until June, 1997, its stock had appreciated more than a hundred-fold. Furthermore, established vendors like AT&T, Nortel and NEC blithely went on their merry way, ignoring the scrappy junk-yard dog from Stanford until they suddenly noticed that Cisco now "owned" the router market.

AT&T and other large companies were just sticking to the knitting, incrementing their way to better products. When the Internet took off as a market and small companies needed routers in their offices, Cisco was there with the right products at the right time, and entire markets were snatched from under the noses of the established market leaders.

The Cisco story is not unique. While it is increasingly common to find revolutionary companies springing out of college dorm rooms, many organizations have great butterfly farms in their own facilities, and *still* miss the opportunities. In the next chapter we'll talk about the research on new product development done by Harvard Business School professor, Clayton Christensen. He studied the computer disk-drive industry and discovered that each new breakthrough in drive capacity and miniaturization took place within existing disk-drive companies; yet they almost always failed to see the merit in these developments.

Education, on the surface, seems almost impervious to butterflies. Many classrooms today would be recognizable to educators from the late 19th century. The last butterfly to impact education was probably the mass-produced book; and even this development took over one hundred years to make its mark.

We live in a different world now. Technology of all kinds is commonplace, and is well understood by today's youth. Today's children are not from Generation X, they are from Generation.com.

In college education, we are starting to see some transformations taking place with the rise of "virtual" universities. These electronic universities are generally started by existing brick-and-mortar institutions as a way of protecting their future — a good idea. Yet many of them are simply placing old wine in new bottles. The underlying idea of scope and sequence in class design (a concept suited for the world of linear time) is preserved in many course offerings, even though other models might be more appropriate in this chaotic age. But colleges and universities are at least exploring alternative models.

This is rarely the case in the world of K-12 education, even though some experiments have shown great potential. One educational butterfly that is now a decade old is called the Buddy System. This Indiana-based project has placed computers with modems and printers in the homes of seven thousand children throughout the state. Schools from all over the state are involved with this project: high-income, low-income, urban, rural — you name it.

Because the teachers at the Buddy schools know that *every* child has a computer at home, this home-based technology is built into the lesson planning. As a result, when the kids go home, they log onto the network and take part in collaborative projects and assignments with their peers all over the state. This activity has replaced TV watching for many kids, and has had the effect of adding the equivalent of thirty days to the school year without keeping the school doors open one extra day.

As for the cost, consider this. Texas spends about $450 per student every year on textbooks. For about three times this amount you could purchase a laptop computer, with a modem and printer, that would last quite a few years. We could, if we chose, bring powerful technology into the hands of every student in the country, and save money while increasing academic performance.

Hunting Butterflies

How should we keep on the lookout for butterflies? It is hard because the forces leading to a revolution can be quite small at first. One of the characteristics of new paradigms is that they grow exponentially. They start off slowly — so slowly at first that they often sail beneath our perceptual radar. When they do emerge into our awareness, they are often growing so fast that we can feel overwhelmed.

Remember when we were told that oat bran was good for us? It seemed that, overnight, the dietary habits of a nation were changed as we stuffed ourselves with as much bran as possible. In fact, had we looked closely, the seeds of this revolution (no pun intended) had been sown a long time before.

How do we go about raising your awareness of potential butterflies? Our lives seem so preoccupied by the tyranny of the urgent that we scarcely have time to look at anything outside our narrow range of view. Yet, if we don't spend some time peering around the future's edge, we'll likely miss the birth of butterflies that can have a tremendous impact on our organizations.

For me, the task is full-time. I subscribe to over two-dozen magazines, newsletters and other documents that arrive in my mailbox every month. Most of these relate to specific industries I'm interested in, but several of them cover a wide range of topics. I find myself continually challenged by publications with an attitude: magazines like *Upside*, *Red Herring*, *WIRED*, *etc.* In addition, I also subscribe to several on-line services that provide me with daily briefings in areas I'm interested in. A quick scan of these briefings lets me know if there is something I need to check more closely, so this task only takes a few minutes each day.

It takes time to develop your internal mechanism for catching an interesting idea on the fly, but, with practice, this is a skill you can develop.

There are lots of great ways to maintain awareness of new developments, and new tools for this task are being developed daily. One of the "antique" technologies of value is the audio cassette tape. Think about it, audio is the only informational medium you can use while you are doing something else (like driving to work). All kinds of monthly programs are made available on audio cassette, and you can use these tools during the time you are driving.

I've become quite disciplined about reading. I'm on airplanes almost every week, so I always take a pile of magazines with me. I rip out the articles I need to read in depth and throw the rest away. (The flight crews "love" me for leaving all my trash on the plane, although I am generally pretty good about carrying my junk to the garbage can myself).

The question you need to ask yourself is this: "In this time of rapid change, can I afford *not* to keep up with new developments that might obliterate my organization if I ignore them?"

Activities for this chapter:

1. What *small* changes are taking place in your field of expertise that could upset your apple cart? Make a list of these changes, and then think about whether your organization can move to take advantage of these changes through incremental approaches, or if a revolution is called for. Finally, think about the consequences of *not* paying attention to these changes. Will your organization be able to survive if these small butterflies continue to grow?

2. What strategies do you have for keeping yourself up to date on developments in your field of expertise? What magazines, newsletters, on-line newsgroups, and specialty web sites exist to help you with this task? Make a list of these informational sources and then develop a plan for butterfly hunting every day.

From Diminishing Returns to Increasing Returns

Them that's got, gets.
— Anonymous

The previous chapter described the power of the butterfly effect on institutions. In this chapter, we'll explore the emergence of strange attractors.

To get us started on this topic, let's look at a traditional concept from economics: the law of diminishing returns. Basically, it states that as an industry grows based on the popularity of a particular product, it will increase its use of resources until the cost of the product equals the price the companies making it receive. This law operates in industries characterized by congealed physical resources with little informational content.

An alternative economic viewpoint has been developed by Stanford Professor W. Brian Arthur (now at the Santa Fe Institute), who developed the theory of *increasing* returns to explain a phenomenon that takes hold in industries characterized by congealed knowledge with little physical content. In a paper he wrote for *Harvard Business Review*, "Increasing Returns and the Two Worlds of Business" (July/August, 1996: 100-109) he says the following:

> Our understanding of how markets and businesses operate was passed down to us more than a century ago by a handful of European economists — Alfred Marshall in England and a few of his contemporaries on the continent. It is an understanding based squarely upon the assumption of diminishing returns: products or companies that get ahead in a market eventually run into limitations, so that a predictable equilibrium of prices and market shares is reached. The theory was in rough measure valid for the bulk-processing, smokestack economy of Marshall's day. And it still thrives

27

in today's economics textbooks. But steadily and continuously in this century, Western economies have undergone a transformation from bulk-material manufacturing to design and use of technology — from processing of resources to processing of information, from application of raw energy to application of ideas. As this shift has taken place, the underlying mechanisms that determine economics behavior have shifted from ones of diminishing to ones of *increasing* returns.

The basic idea behind increasing returns is that there is a positive feedback loop that gets set into motion to perpetuate the success of a market leader, causing the leader to pull further ahead as the competition falls further and further behind. This mechanism of positive feedback results in a "lock-in" position very similar to a strange attractor — a very slight force can tip the scale one way or another in the beginning, but once you are locked in, it is very hard to find a way out.

To take one example, consider the arrangement of keys on your computer keyboard. Unless you have modified the keyboard yourself, the top row of letter keys starts with QWERTY. This pattern (often called "qwerty") defines the Sholes keyboard arrangement — a keyboard layout dating back to the early days of mechanical typewriters.

The first practical typewriter was invented by Christopher Latham Sholes, and was marketed by the Remington Arms company in 1873. The action of the type bars in the early typewriters was very sluggish, and tended to jam frequently. Sholes obtained a list of the most common letters used in English, and rearranged his keyboard from an alphabetic arrangement to one in which the most common letters were spread fairly far apart on the keyboard. Since typists at that time used the "hunt-and-peck" method, Sholes' arrangement increased the time it took for the typists to hit any two consecutive keys enough to ensure that each type bar had time to fall back before the next one came up. Sholes hadn't imagined that typing would ever be faster than handwriting, which is usually around 20 words per minute or less.
In fact, Sholes claimed he had designed the worst keyboard for typing English. (When I was at the Xerox Palo Alto Research Center in the 1970's, we disproved Sholes' hypothesis using a theoretical analysis of keyboard layouts. His keyboard is *not* the worst, but it is in the lowest quartile).

The typewriter became successful (although not for many years) and this arrangement of keys became locked into use, long after type bar jams ceased to be a problem.

In the meantime, much better keyboard arrangements were developed. One of them, the Dvorak Simplified Keyboard, is so good that it is used by most of the people who hold the records for speed typing.

So, why haven't we changed?

The answer appears to be that typing takes sufficiently long to learn that experienced typists can't afford to take the time to switch from one layout to the other. Instead, most (but not all) typists persist in using a sub-optimal keyboard layout.

Professor Arthur mentions other examples of increasing returns: Computer operating systems, for example. In the early to mid 1980's three operating systems were in use: CP/M, DOS, and Apple's Macintosh. One of these (DOS) was clearly inferior, yet it became the standard. Why? Because it was adopted by IBM (and the clone manufacturers). Once a slight lead was established, software developers had an incentive to support the front runner. This caused more people to gravitate toward that platform, thus further incentivizing software developers. The resulting positive feedback loop caused DOS (and now Windows) to assume a lead position, even though they are clearly inferior to other choices.

These examples are not meant to imply that all strange attractors are bad. They merely demonstrate that the power of an installed base can, *by itself* determine success in a marketplace.

With this quick overview of Arthur's work in hand, let's explore the kinds of markets and organizations for which strange attractors based on increasing returns can thrive. As I mentioned before:

- **Diminishing returns apply for organizations, industries and products characterized by congealed physical resources with little informational content.**

- **Increasing returns apply for organizations, industries and products characterized by congealed information with little physical content.**

Industries based on material goods obey the law of diminishing returns, while knowledge-based industries can obey the law of increasing returns.

What are some examples of increasing returns industries? Computer software is probably the largest one in existence today. All the value is in the information. The cost of goods is quite small (a CD-ROM costs under a dollar to manufacture), and the cost can be driven down even further if software is distributed over the Internet.

The microprocessor industry is another one benefiting from increasing returns. While this industry might, at first glance, be thought of as producing physical goods, the value in a computer chip is its instruction set — its information.

How does a company succeed in an increasing returns world? By getting in front of customers as quickly as possible. As the Canadian futurist Frank Ogden states, "It used to be that success came to those who got in on the ground floor. Today you have to get in on the excavation."

Imagine the following scenario: A manager of a company in the 1960's suggests giving away a million copies of the company's only product to secure a strong market share. How long would that person be given to clear out his or her desk? And yet that is exactly what Netscape did just a few years ago when it was one of many companies introducing software for exploring the World-Wide-Web. As a result, Netscape established an early lead that has only recently been challenged by Microsoft (in a way we will describe in a later chapter).

Any organization or business based on networks is also a candidate for increasing returns. The reason for this is that the old concept that scarcity increases value is turned upside down in a network economy.

Traditionally, we think that scarcity breeds value — the more rare something is, the more it is likely to cost (assuming demand outstrips supply). In a network economy, we have a new law:

The Law of the Network Economy...
Ubiquity breeds value.

This counter-intuitive idea is fairly easy to demonstrate. Imagine yourself being approached by a fax machine salesperson in the early 1970's. At that time, you'd probably be shown a Xerox Telecopier capable of sending a page of text across the country in a mere six minutes. Before you scoff at the speed, remember there was no Federal Express then, and many large firms used private courier services to get documents across the country, at great expense.

The fax machine would have had great value except for one tiny problem: the installed base was so small that you were unlikely to find other people to whom you could send faxes. One of the reasons for this is that fax machines were not only a fairly new concept, they were very expensive. At that time, fax machines were scarce and they had little value.

Fast-forward to today. Fax machines are ubiquitous and cheap. They have tremendous value, and the value of your fax machine increases every time someone else purchases one. The reason for this is that the network of people with whom you can exchange faxes has grown. Furthermore, the less expensive fax machines are to purchase, the more people will buy them, thus increasing the value of the network even more.

Bob Metcalfe, inventor of the Ethernet, formulated what is now called Metcalfe's Law:

> **The power of a network increases by the square of the number of users.**
> **— Bob Metcalfe**

To see Metcalfe's Law in action, look at the tremendous expansion of the Internet. This communication system was originally designed as a fault-tolerant way to transmit data for the military. As the Internet opened up to access by anyone with a personal computer, it started to grow in size exponentially over time. As a result we now live in a world where e-mail far outstrips mail delivered by the post office. In 1997 the U. S. Postal Service delivered 195 billion pieces of mail. During that same year the Electronic Messaging Association estimates that 2.7 *trillion* e-mail messages were sent.

To see the impact of networks on your life, look at some of your old business cards. A long time ago, all they had was your address and phone number. Then they also had your fax number. Later, they included your e-mail address, and, today, many people have their Web sites listed.

How can you decide if your organization or industry is susceptible to increasing returns?

Here are the starting points:

Are you engaged in knowledge-based activities? Can you take advantage of networks?

If the answer to either of these questions is "Yes," then you need to think about your capacity to jump-start your position in the market to get as many early adopters of your product or service as possible. Rather than starting with high margins that become lower over time (the diminishing returns model), you start with low margins that grow over time as you establish a lock-in position.

Educational institutions are clear candidates for increasing returns — they are in the knowledge industry, and they have a loose set of standards that promote networks. For example, national frameworks exist for mathematics, English, social studies, *etc.* Even better, schools (along with prisons and mental hospitals) are the only places where, if you don't go, someone comes and gets you.

The lock-in of schools seems quite secure, and for this reason it is imperative that educational systems constantly strive to insure they are meeting the needs of their students. In a diminishing returns world, excellence would be achieved through competition. As the lessons with DOS and QWERTY show, no such guarantee of excellence is assured in the world of increasing returns.

Fortunately, vocal parents, educators and students are continuing to pressure schools to change in ways that insure that our students are prepared for their future, not for our past.

Before leaving this chapter, I want to explore one of the danger points of increasing returns: the power of the installed base. Harvard Professor Clayton Christensen wrote an excellent book, *The Innovator's Dilemma: When New Technologies Cause Great Firms to Fail.* He studied companies that were excellent at what they did, yet seemed totally incapable of making the transformation to a new product line when technology improved. He studied the computer disk drive industry in depth and found, almost without exception, that the advances leading to faster, smaller disk drives with greater capacity were created within companies that were industry leaders. Yet, these companies refused to develop the new technology and, when it finally came to market, the established companies often went bankrupt.

It is easy, with hindsight, to say that these companies behaved stupidly, but Christensen shows that they were victims of the power of the installed base. Imagine a researcher asking for the financial resources needed to take a new product, for which there is no current demand, from the lab to the marketplace. At the same time, a manager of an existing product line is asking for those same resources to be used in support of existing products for which there is a large, established market. Without the benefit of the long view, it's easy to see who will get the resources. The group with the new idea will get frustrated, leave and start a competing company — often driving their former employer to the brink of bankruptcy when the new technology finally takes off.

This cautionary tale has applications in industries and organizations of all types. While lock-in can provide security, it can also breed complacency. As educational consultant Gil Noble says; "The single greatest enemy of excellence is 'good enough'."

Activities for this chapter:

1. What strange attractors do you see in your organization? How many of these are productive? How many are not? How can you effect change in your organization when you have large forces to overcome?

2. Think about your organization, company or industry. Does it meet the criteria for increasing returns? Can you envision a strategy for increasing your dominance in the marketplace?

3. Listen carefully to how new ideas are treated in staff meetings. Are they being "shot down"? Is the power of the installed base limiting your organization's vision? How can you encourage your co-workers to take a longer-term view of innovations that might not pay off right away?

From Focus
to Peripheral Vision

Where a calculator on the ENIAC is equipped with 18,000 vacuum tubes and weighs 30 tons, computers in the future might have only 1,000 vacuum tubes and perhaps only weigh 1 1/2 tons.
— Popular Mechanics, March 1949, two years after the invention of the transistor.

In 1860, a stage coach and freight company owner by the name of William Russell had an idea on how to improve the transportation of mail from Missouri to California. At that time it took about eight weeks for mail to make it around the Cape into California. Alternatively, the mail could be sent by overland stage which took as long as 20 days.

What Russell had in mind was something far more efficient. He designed the Pony Express and created a service that was the absolute best at what they did. Instead of taking eight weeks to get messages to California the Pony Express could deliver mail in as little as eight days. In fact the record was 7.5 days — the time it took to get Lincoln's inaugural address from St. Joseph, Missouri to Sacramento, California.

But even though the Pony Express was the absolute best at what it did, it was not good enough. In 1861 the telegraph line was finally extended from the Mississippi River to California and the Pony Express ceased to exist.

Mail that used to take eight weeks and then (through the Pony Express) eight days could now be transmitted to California in four hours at a speed of 18 bits per second. The fact that the Pony Express was the absolute best of what they did was not important. They still became obsolete.

This is an important message. You can be the very best and what you do, but unless you pay attention to competing technologies you can be put out of business very easily.

Was Russell caught by surprise with the telegraph? He shouldn't have been. Telegraphy was a mature technology by 1860. The problem was more likely that he did not think of the telegraph as competition — to Russell, mail was a physical entity to be carried, not data to be transmitted.

Challenges of this sort confront businesses every day. In their quest to be better than their competition, they define their competitors too narrowly. The results can be tragic for those who stay too focused. For example, in a 1977 speech to the World Future Society, Ken Olsen, founder of Digital Equipment Corporation said: "There is no reason for any individual to have a computer in the home."

History has proven Olsen wrong, and the acquisition of DEC by Compaq in 1998 sends a message to all who define the scope of their business too narrowly.

The challenge is quite severe. Remember that the Pony Express was the absolute *best* at what they did, yet they still went out of business.

What other kinds of businesses can be affected? The danger of keeping too narrow a focus can cripple anyone. Consider the airlines, for example. I'm sure most carriers would define their competition pretty narrowly, listing other airlines and stopping there. To make my point, I'm going to suggest that the airlines have another competitor to contend with: Kinko's.

That's right, Kinko's, the 24-hour copy shops that are expanding their services to include videoconferencing. Instead of flying across the country to take part in a one-hour business meeting, a participant could go to a local videoconferencing center and take part in the meeting remotely. The cost would be less than the airfare in most cases, and the participants would not have to lose a day or more in travel time.

As of mid-1998, videoconferencing has not achieved sufficient popularity to be much of a threat to business travel, but the potential consequences are so great that airlines should be thinking about it today. Here's why. Business travelers generally pay full-fares. They don't have the luxury of making their ticket reservations far in advance, and they don't usually stay out over the weekends. The fares paid by these travelers, in effect, subsidize the sporadic vacation traveler who gets to fly round-trip for $50 and three Taco Bell wrappers.

An enterprising airline that wants to remain in business might think about broadening its services to meet the needs of its customers in new ways. If videoconferencing is going to become more popular in the future, why not create videoconferencing rooms in their airport club rooms? These rooms could be rented out, and catering services could be provided for lunch meetings, *etc.* These videoconferencing centers could be located in hub airports: Chicago, San Francisco, New York, or Rio de Janeiro. Flights that feed into these hubs could carry participants who live in outlying areas. They would travel to the closest hub to take part in a meeting, and could still get home that night.

The convenience of this service would probably make it quite profitable, and it would build brand loyalty for those times where business travelers need to fly long distances.

This proposal requires that the airlines develop their peripheral vision — their capacity to look beyond their current service and to think about alternative ways of meeting their clients' needs.

It might seem I'm picking on the airlines, but I'm not. (It is true that this chapter is being written as I fly from San Francisco to Chicago, but that is not the point). *Every* industry and service needs to develop its peripheral vision in this era of accelerated change. As the Pony Express learned, you can be the very best at what you do, and still be put out of business if your focus is too narrow.

I think the challenge of developing peripheral vision can be expressed this way: organizations need to be able to identify their *true* competitors. These competitors will include others in your current field, as well as those in other fields who have the ability to meet your customers' needs in new ways.

How do you go about identifying these new competitors? One tool you can learn comes from the field of Value Engineering. It is called the Function Analysis System Technique, or FAST diagramming developed by Charles Bytheway. (I am indebted to Ron Voth for introducing me to this concept).

The goal of the FAST diagram is to find the Highest Order Function of your enterprise. While FAST diagramming was developed to allow the function analysis of a single product or service, it works well for organizations. (For more information on FAST diagramming, visit the web site (http://www.value-eng.com) of the Society of American Value Engineers.)

You start the process by describing your current product or service with a verb-noun pair. Try to use a quantitative noun and active verb when possible. For example, someone from the US Postal Service might start with the function: Deliver Letters. You put this function in a box at the right side of a sheet of paper. Next, to the left of this box, you put another one containing a verb-noun pair that increases the abstraction of the right-most box. This box contains the answer to the question "Why?"

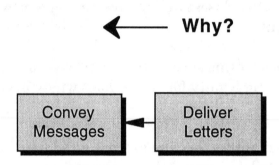

For example, you might put Convey Messages in this box. This process is repeated, adding boxes to the left, until you have reached the highest order function of interest to you. This function is your goal.

If you move from left to right along this diagram, you'll see that each box to the right answers the question, "How?" For that reason, this diagram is sometimes called a How/Why diagram.

Originally, FAST diagramming was used as a tool to help improve value and reduce unnecessary costs. It focused especially on the *how* of things, with arrows going from left-to-right along a critical path. I'm more interested in its use as a powerful *strategic* tool, helping you develop your peripheral vision regarding your business or profession by emphasizing the *why*. By showing the arrows pointing from right to left along a yet-to-be identified Critical Path, FAST diagramming becomes a strategic, long-view tool.

There are many ways to go about creating these diagrams. One way to start is to just make a list of verb-noun pairs that describe the functions of your organization's products or services. One you have this list you can build your diagram by comparing these verb-noun pairs with the others in your list. Ones that answer the question "Why?" should be placed to the left of ones that answer "How?"

Let's explore this with an example. What are some functions of the postal service? Here's a list I came up with (although you should create your own as well):

Deliver Mail
Deliver Letters
Transmit Information
Convey Messages
Exchange Data

Next, you might want to place each verb-noun pair on a Post-It™ note so they can be moved around easily. The next step is to arrange them in the proper order. For example, delivering mail is a higher-order function than delivering (physical) letters, so it should be placed to the left of delivering letters. By continuing with this process (which will probably require moving some notes that have been moved already), you'll have a completed diagram.

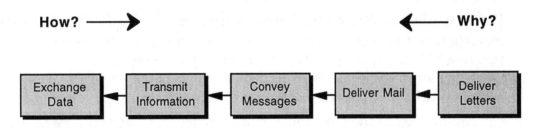

At this point, the highest order function is to the far left. To see how your organization does its task today, just read the chart from left to right. If this doesn't flow properly, then you need to work on the diagram some more. You may have left out some functions, or have some of them in the wrong order.

Once you are finished, you have a very powerful result: you'll have identified the starting point for finding "new" competitors — businesses, products or services that have the potential to render your current product or service line obsolete. Because you'll be identifying these potential competitors early, you'll be able to think about how to incorporate them into your activity to insure your future growth.

For example, my list for the postal service has Exchange Data as their highest order function. (You might have another response, but it will probably be similar). Any list of competitors for the postal service would have to include UPS, FedEx, and other suppliers of services for the delivery of physical items such as letters. But, it would also have to include anyone in the business of exchanging data. This would include the telephone companies, the Internet, and a wide variety of new and emerging technologies.

Any organization wishing to stay in business today needs to have two types of competitive analysis going on. The first is the traditional sort that focuses on alternative providers for the function at the right side of your FAST diagram. The other is watching what is happening in the area defined by your highest order function. Once you've started developing you peripheral vision, you'll want to start watching for developments in these peripheral industries to see what impact they can have on you. Your organization will probably want to start investing in some of these areas in order to remain competitive.

To illustrate the kind of technology that the postal service, FedEx and others should be watching today, look at the emerging field of rapid prototyping. This is a technology that uses a computer controlled laser beam to form incredibly complex parts out of light-hardened polymers. Basically, a digital data file sent over the Internet from an office in San Francisco can control a laser fabricator halfway around the world. Prototype parts that once required an overnight courier to get them from one location to another, can now be fabricated from data files sent over the Internet for the price of a local phone call.

Once you start working with FAST diagrams as strategic tools, you'll be amazed at the new opportunities you'll see opening up for your organization.

Activities for this chapter:

1. Create a Function Analysis System Technique diagram to identify the highest order function of your organization or profession. A worksheet for this is provided at the end of the book.

   A. First create a list of active verb-descriptive noun pairs that describe the various functions of your activity.

   B. Next, arrange them in sequence in order of decreasing abstraction from left to right.

   C. When you are done, enter the verb-noun pairs on the worksheet. If you've done the task properly, each box to the left answers "Why?" and each box to the right answers "How?" The left-most box represents the highest-order function of your enterprise.

2. Once you have identified a highest-order function for your organization, make a list of alternative providers of this function, since they are your new competition. How many of these new competitors were previously unknown to you? How many of them have ideas you can incorporate in your existing organization? What strategies can you develop to increase awareness of these competing forces within your organization?

From Just-in-Case to Just-in-Time

Context is King.
— Jim Brazell

Dell computer has some of the most modern factories in the world. They were a pioneer in the field of electronic commerce, and, in early 1998, their Web site generated several million dollars of sales per day. When customers order a Dell computer, they are dealing directly with the factory. Furthermore, each computer is built to order and the time lag from order to delivery is a mere four or five days.

How can a company provide a wide range of semi-customized products and deliver them in a timely fashion?

By not having any inventory.

Each Dell computer is an example of mass-customization. Rather than build a stockpile of computers held in inventory until they are sold (the old "just-in-case" model), Dell builds computers "just-in-time." This requires close relationships with suppliers to insure that the raw parts needed for each computer are delivered quickly. The benefit, both to the customer and the manufacturer, can be tremendous — especially in a fast-moving field like personal computers.

In the traditional manufacturing world where articles are manufactured based on projected demand, and then stored in warehouses until they are purchased, companies were penalized for introducing new models with the latest features if they had any old models in stock. Yet, if they ran out of a

43

popular model, this upset customers who then looked for alternate suppliers. This careful balancing of inventory required a lot of guessing on the part of those who scheduled items for manufacturing. Some companies, like Apple Computer, consistently underestimated the popularity of some products (such as the PowerBook laptops) and overestimated the popularity of others, requiring the sale of old inventory at heavily discounted prices when a new product line was introduced.

With advances in computer technology appearing every few months, any company with a large inventory of unsold computers can find the value of this inventory declining rapidly when a vendor (such as Intel) introduces yet another faster microprocessor.

Just-in-time manufacturing addresses this challenge by tightening the loop between the parts supplier and the manufacturer, and between the manufacturer and the customer. By having fresh components delivered as orders come in, the product line is "future-proofed," since product upgrades can be introduced immediately. By disintermediating the relationship with the customer, the manufacturer does not have to worry about unsold goods sitting in some distributor's warehouse.

The high-tech industry is not alone in finding the merits of just-in-time manufacturing. The automotive industry is moving quickly into this domain as well, and is relying on network technologies (such as corporate Intranets) to facilitate the process. Ford Motor Company, for example, connects some 120,000 workstations at offices and factories around the world to thousands of Ford Web sites with proprietary information. Their product development system, for example, which documents thousands of steps in manufacturing, assembling, and testing vehicles, is updated hourly. This application allows Ford to trim the time needed to get a new model into production from 36 months to 24 months.

They are also moving closer to just-in-time manufacturing, a process requiring the coordination of the delivery of thousands of parts. By opening their network to suppliers, part orders can be more closely coupled with production schedules. The impact can be tremendous. In 1996, for example, it took more than 50 days to get a Mustang of your choice delivered from the plant to the dealer. In 1998 it took 15 days. By the end of 1999, it will be even faster, saving billions of dollars in current inventory and fixed costs.

The model of just-in-time manufacturing has a lot of benefits. It allows companies to reduce or eliminate inventory costs, it allows them to introduce new products quickly without having to worry about selling off old inventory, and it facilitates mass-customization where each product is made to a customer's specification.

Prior to the invention of mass-production, the making of goods was a craft. Items were made to order by craftsmen. Each was unique, and expensive to manufacture. This changed with the development of mass-production. Mass production was a hallmark of the industrial age. It was facilitated by the division of labor into small chunks of activities that could be handled by relatively unskilled workers (as opposed to the previous craft model of manufacturing where an entire product was the work of a single person). It also supported the idea of interchangeable parts, so that repairs could be made easily in the field. Most importantly, uniformity reduced costs, making mass-produced goods affordable.

Eli Whitney's invention of mass-production set the stage for a lot of important developments that brought the industrial revolution to full flower throughout the world. When products were mass-produced in high volume, they could be made cheaply, thus increasing the potential pool of customers. Ford's adoption of Whitney's ideas transformed the automotive industry, and helped trigger incredible economic growth.

The rapid rise of information technologies has now facilitated the latest transformation illustrated with our opening examples: the move from mass production to mass customization. Mass customization retains many of the cost benefits of mass production (even improving on them in some cases), while affording the opportunity for people to purchase unique products. Levi's, for example, has a line called Personal Pair jeans for women. These jeans are made to order and are delivered to a local store for pickup in a few days. While customers are willing to pay more for a custom pair of jeans, the fully-burdened manufacturing cost to Levi's is probably less than that associated with making a pair of jeans for the rack.

Mass customization requires a shift to just-in-time manufacturing. But the concept of moving from just-in-case to just-in-time is not limited to manufacturing. It has application in other areas as well, including education.

The school system of my youth reflected the paradigms of the time. Just as factories were based on mass-production and just-in-case models of manufacturing, our schools were places where learning took on a just-in-case format as well.

Evidence of this abounds. Students in my time often asked teachers, "Why do I need to know this?" The response was, "Because it will be on the test," or

"Because you'll need to know this later in life." In other words, we were taught things just in case we'd need them later.

The result was that we often were exposed to a lot of learning that took place devoid of context. We learned early that content was king, and we became masters of what my colleague Ian Jukes refers to as the "bulimic" curriculum where we binged and purged. Our teachers taught us a lot of material that we retained just long enough to give back on a test, after which we quickly forgot it in order to make room for new material.

Intellectual anorexia was the order of the day.

To illustrate this, assuming you are of my generation (50+), answer this question taken from one of my high-school U. S. History tests:

> *One of the major battles in the War of 1812 was fought in New Orleans. When was the battle fought, and what made it significant?*

(If you chose 1812 as the year, go to the back of the class. If, by remembering the old popular song about the Battle of New Orleans, you chose 1814, join those in the back of the class. Both of these answers are wrong).

Here's another question (from mathematics):

> *Find the square root of 473,285 to the nearest integer. Show all steps in your calculation. (You may not use logarithm tables to perform this calculation).*

Well, class, how did you do? Did you ace this test? There was a time in your life when your teachers thought you needed to learn this stuff (otherwise why teach and test it?)

Please don't get me wrong, history is a wonderful thing to study, and the War of 1812 was a tragic conflict in so many ways that we all should understand it and learn from it. By the same token, square roots are important, and we should all have effective ways of finding them when we need to (even though today we'd probably all pull out our two-dollar calculators). My point has nothing to do with the intrinsic value of the content, only that many of us have lost our memory of this content, probably because we did not have a clear *context* in mind when we learned it.

One characteristic of just-in-case learning is that it is built on the idea that content is King. In today's fast-paced world, this is a dangerous notion. As my friend Jim Brazell says, content is *not* King, context is.

If we are going to have our young people learning information in this era of rapid change, it is increasingly important that context be the driving force, not content.

This suggests a shift in learning from just-in-case to just-in-time.

Of course, this approach flies in the face of the linear model of time that produced factory whistles (and school bells at the end of periods), and a curriculum based on a rigid scope and sequence. Just-in-case learning fits well with lecture-based instruction, and this ties in effectively with the tragic reality of secondary school where teachers have over 100 students and teach several periods of the same class. Our buildings, class schedules, and just about everything else in our educational system is quite well suited to the just-in-case delivery model for education. The only part that doesn't fit well in this model are the teachers, students and their respective needs.

And therein lies the problem.

In a world moving at light-speed, "facts" change with great rapidity. Ask medical doctors how quickly things are changing in their profession. Ask tax attorneys how often they need to return to classes to keep up. Engineers live in such a rapidly changing world that their education is continuous and ongoing. Increasingly, we are finding ourselves in a position where learning and work are virtually one and the same thing.

So, if we are going to be learning throughout our lives, it seems that the shift from just-in-case to just-in-time is essential. Corporate training departments have known this for a long time, and many corporations are in a constant search for new educational tools to facilitate the formal and informal learning that makes up an increasing part of their employees' days.

For those teaching in the K-12 arena, a few tasks emerge.

1. Foster the development of productive habits of mind for problem solving and information finding,
2. Develop student capacity to locate relevant information,
3. Provide students with the tools they need to verify the accuracy of the information they find,
4. Give students lots of opportunities to coalesce and make meaning from this information, and
5. Help them develop the communication strategies they need to demonstrate their learning in the context of a specific problem being solved.

The key, quite simply, is to create an environment in which rigor *and* relevance are treated with equal respect, not as tradeoffs.

How do we do all this — especially given the constraints of a State-mandated curriculum?

I think the challenge is not to change *what* we teach as much as it is to change *how* we teach. We can still expect students to achieve mastery of the subjects, but we can change the instructional methods in ways that foster the development of problem-solving skills, and that take advantage of modern tools for research and evaluation.

For years we have been talking about the need for lifelong learning, yet we also talk about K-12, college, and workforce training as separate entities. One way to think about a lifelong learning environment is to imagine the creation of Educational Maintenance Organizations (EMO's) that people can use whenever they need to acquire a new skill. An EMO would be similar to an HMO and "coverage" might be paid for by employers and employees together through tax exempt contributions.

Many large companies have excellent staff development facilities on-site where EMO services would continue to be provided for their employees. Smaller companies that don't have on-site staff development could take advantage of local community colleges or other educational institutions to meet the needs of their employees.

The greatest benefit of employee access to an EMO comes when someone is changing jobs and/or employers. When large companies lay off a large number of workers, the severance package rarely includes educational options so these people can acquire the new skills needed by new employers. If each individual had his or her own EMO coverage, this would facilitate the kind of just-in-time education needed to prepare people for new job opportunities.

I already mentioned that community colleges would be perfect delivery mechanisms for this service in many communities, but they are not the only choice. Private trade schools are already in this business (although without the "insurance" metaphor) and the World-Wide-Web is an ideal delivery mechanism for many kinds of just-in-time learning services. Sun Microsystems, for example, has moved the bulk of their staff development to the Web to save on travel costs, but this move had the added benefit of supporting just-in-time learning. Part of Sun's efforts are available to the general public for free through www.sun.com/sunergy, if you wish to check it out.

Recent advances in Web-based conferencing tools (such as mShow from www.mshow.com, and RealPresenter from www.realaudio.com) allow slide shows to be delivered over dial-up connections to the Web. RealAudio's contribution to audio delivery over the Web has put the inexpensive delivery of audio programming in the hands of everyone with access to a computer. Two-way and multi-point videoconferencing is moving to the desktop and, as bandwidth to the home increases, the potential of the Web as an EMO delivery mechanism will become even greater than it is today.

Activities for this chapter:

1. If you are an instructor at *any* level (either in school or industry), take one topic you teach and answer the following questions:

   A. What habits of mind are brought into play when students explore this topic (these can be problem solving strategies, communication strategies, need-finding strategies, *etc.*).
   B. What are the likely tools that students will use to locate relevant information?
   C. How will students verify the accuracy of the information they find?
   D. How will students make meaning from this information and relate it in context with their lives or job-related tasks?
   E. How will the things they have learned be communicated effectively, and applied in the course of their work or future studies?
   F. What evaluative tools will you apply to answer the previous questions?

From Physics to Biology

Consistency is the hobgoblin of tiny minds.
— Ralph Waldo Emerson

The industrial era, characterized by a linear model of time, was also dominated by metaphors based on physics. We talked about businesses that ran like a well-oiled machine, of processes that ran like clockwork, *etc.* Coupled with these metaphors was a reductionist approach to thinking that implied human control over all processes. Organizations were built around the concept of command and control, with hierarchical structures and a clear chain of command.

Because of the perceived need for central control of an organization, many companies built up sets of rules that were propagated to all members of the group. These complex rules dictated behavior. They also had another consequence: Complex rules often resulted in simple (and simplistic) behavior. If you doubt this, try ordering an egg sandwich from any major fast-food restaurant at two in the afternoon — you can't get one. Is this because they ran out of eggs and muffins? No — it is because the behavior of your favorite fast-food restaurant is dictated by a complex set of rules that state what food items will be available when. To violate these rules is to violate the essence of the organization: namely that management has more to say about the operation of the restaurant than the customers do.

Fast-food restaurants are not the only ones. I recently withdrew some frequent flyer miles from my account to get a ticket to New York. The meeting I was scheduled to attend was canceled, so I called the airline's service desk to have the miles put back in my account. I was told that this would cost me

$75. Since the meeting had been moved to New Orleans, I asked if the ticket could be switched to a New Orleans flight. I was told that this would also cost me $75, but that I could reschedule the trip to New York for a later time at no cost. I pointed out that it took as much work to reissue a New York ticket as it did to change my flight to New Orleans, but the person on the phone held tightly to the rules.

This blind adherence to corporate rules characterizes the command and control structures of a company using physical metaphors of operation. The underlying force in such organizations is Newtonian. An object in motion remains in motion unless acted upon by an external force. Command and control companies have been pretty good at resisting external forces until now. But, because of the butterfly effect, small forces can turn into tornadoes overnight, and when they do, entire organizations can be swept away.

Structures based on physical metaphors resulted in management systems in which information flowed from level to level, often at a snail's pace. While the stability and strength implied by these structures may have served industries in a time of less rapid change, they do not work so well in the fast-moving non-linear world of today. The idea that stable organizations were the result of a clear set of commands from a central source was an artifact of this mechanical view of the world. And yet, all around us, the world was teeming with self-organizing structures that had no clear leader — bird flocks, ant colonies, and other complex biological systems common to nature. One of the positive consequences of self-organizing natural systems is their incredible tolerance for disruption. Anyone who has tried to entice ants to locate somewhere outside their kitchen knows, first hand, how resilient these biological systems can be.

The new sciences of chaos and complexity theory emerged to explain self-organizing systems, and a new rule emerged: simple rules could lead to incredibly complex behavior. We already saw one aspect of this when we explored strange attractors. The Sierpinski gasket is an incredibly complex object that is produced by the random application of very simple rules (place a dot midway between the previously drawn dot and one of three randomly chosen corners of a triangle. As with the contrast between the world of diminishing and increasing returns, we have a new set of rules:

Physical metaphors lead to complex rules that result in simple and simplistic behavior.

Biological metaphors lead to simple rules that result in complex behavior.

Add to this the incredible resilience of biological systems, and the power of this metaphor for the creation of 21st century businesses and organizations of all kinds is tremendous.

One of the pioneers in this field is a gentleman by the name of Dee Hock — the founder of Visa, probably the largest self-organizing business system on the planet (the Internet being the only other large one I know of).

Dee Hock talks about "chaordic" systems — structures that exist on the border of chaos and order. Some of his speeches have been transcribed and can be found on the Net by searching under Dee Hock, or chaord.

In a speech given at the Extension National Leadership Conference in Washington, DC in 1996, he defined "chaord" this way:

> By "chaord" I mean any self-organizing, adaptive, non-linear, complex organism, organization or community, whether physical, biological or social, the behavior of which harmoniously blends characteristics of both order and chaos. Briefly stated, a chaord is any chaotically-ordered complex. Loosely translated to social organizations, it would mean the harmonious blending of competition and cooperation. Loosely translated to education, lifelong and harmonious blending of intellectual and experiential learning.

Why is this kind of structure important to think about today? It is important because of the combined effects of the rapid and non-linear growth of information, coupled with the collapse of the information float. As Hock stated in the speech mentioned above:

> This endless compression of float, whether of money, information, technology or anything else, can be combined and described as the disappearance of "change" float. The time between what was and what is to be; between past and future. Only a few generations ago, the present stretched unaltered, from a distant past to a dim future. Today the past is ever less predictive, the future ever less predictable and the present scarcely exists at all. Everything is change, with one incredibly important exception. There has been no loss of institutional float. Although their size and power have vastly increased, there has been no new idea of organization since the concepts of corporation, nation-state and university emerged a few centuries ago.

As a result of these insights, Dee Hock spearheaded the creation of Visa, an organization with a staff of only three thousand scattered in twenty-one offices in thirteen countries on four continents which coordinates three-quarters of a trillion dollars in business every year, clearing more transactions in a week than the Federal Reserve does in a year.

Whether existing organizations change their metaphors or not, they will be buffeted by the forces of change we've been emphasizing, and those who resist will find themselves presiding over a diminishing empire.

All of this suggests that organizations of all kinds need to look at the underlying metaphors used in everyday speech. How do you talk or think about your organization? What does your organizational chart look like? How is information shared within your organization? How are decisions made regarding customer service? The answers to these kinds of questions will tell you a lot about your organization, and its capacity to thrive in this world of rapid change.

For example, many organizations today are structured around traditional hierarchical organizational charts:

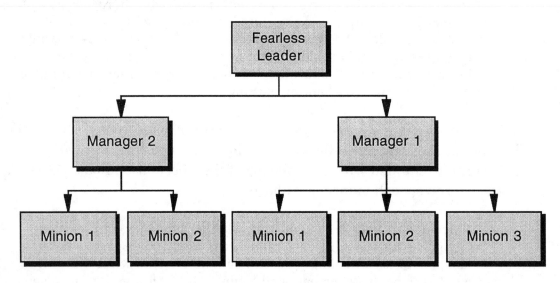

In structures like this, there is a clear chain of command, and the flow of information is often top-down. Even when information moves the other way, it moves through the chain of command. This makes the formation of informal short-term teams difficult. You might have several colleagues at your level with whom you would like to work on a project, but because they are outside your department, you need to go through your supervisor who would talk to the other supervisors until the conversation moved high enough up the chain to reach a person who oversaw all the relevant groups. The request would then filter down through the organization until it reached the right people. This mechanism for collaboration is highly inefficient, and is based on the underlying notion that people further down the chain can't be trusted to interact with peers across organizational boundaries.

An alternative organizational structure is one we employ at the Thornburg Center. Each Associate of our center is a node on a network. Each node has a direct connection to every other one, so if a member of our Canadian team wants to collaborate on a project with our Associate in Berkeley, the two of them negotiate the project together without having to go through any formal request process. As the Director of the Center, I am informed, after the fact, through e-mail.

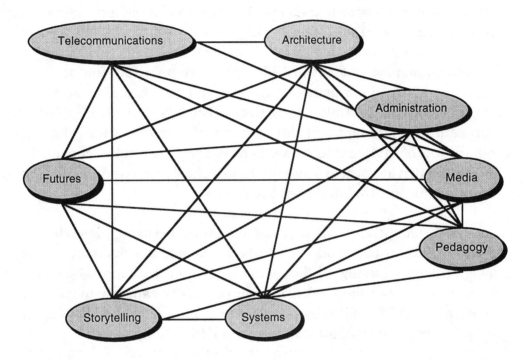

This capacity to establish connections for the duration of a project means that we can be incredibly responsive to new opportunities. Because our Associates are dispersed over several countries, we use e-mail to stay in touch. We have no large staff meetings, although we try to gather in clusters to meet at least once a year. Even so, some of our Associates have never met the entire team.

Notice something interesting about network charts compared with traditional organizational charts:

Organizational chart: people are identified by title
Network chart: people are identified by expertise

In his book, *Out of Control*, author Kevin Kelly talks about the incredible power of network organizations. Since networks are commonplace in nature, their resilience has been tested for millions of years. Kevin states that networks have four important properties: they are distributed, decentralized, collaborative, and adaptive — just like many biological systems.

Distributed businesses have no single location for their business. I sometimes joke that my office is in the Red Carpet Club in Chicago's O'Hare airport.

Decentralization (often called "outsourcing") allows people to focus on their core competency, while farming out other aspects of their business (such as bookkeeping and warehousing) to outsiders. Some schools, for example, outsource their cafeteria and custodial services, allowing them to stay focused on the educational tasks alone.

Collaboration is such a powerful tool, even competitors find it a useful strategy. Many major domestic US airlines, for example, use a reservation system belonging to American Airlines. Such "strategic alliances" are increasingly commonplace today. I know of a private school that offers computer lab privileges to students at the nearby public school, who then allows the private school students to use the gymnasium facility and join athletic teams at the public school.

And, as for adaptivity, the just-in-time manufacturing ideas discussed in the previous chapter are a natural consequence of networks. Concurrent product design involves having all the teams associated with a product working at once to insure its timely release to market. The capacity to respond quickly to changing market conditions — a 21st century survival skill — means that you must follow the flow of information. As Kevin Kelly says,

> A network is a factory for information. As the value of a product is increased by the amount of information invested in it, the networks that engender the knowledge increase in value. A factory-made widget once followed a linear path from design to manufacturing and delivery. Now the biography of a flexibly produced widget becomes a net, distributed over many departments in many places simultaneously, and spilling out beyond the factory, so that it is difficult to say what happens first, or where it happens.

The shift to biological metaphors takes on increased importance as we see evidence of this new paradigm in the marketplace. One example I'd like to share is called the Red Queen.

You may recall, from one of Lewis Carrol's stories, Alice encountering the Red Queen who was running, but not getting anywhere. Alice asked why she was running, and the Red Queen said, "In this world you have to run as fast as you can just to stay still."

The term "Red Queen" is applied in modern biology to describe a relationship between two species which co-evolve in such a way that they, together, obtain a competitive advantage over the other species in their ecosystem. But nature is not the only home to Red Queens.

Look at the market for browser software for the World-Wide-Web. The market is dominated by Netscape and Microsoft. When Netscape entered the market, there were many vendors for browsing software. Netscape took an early lead with an excellent product. Microsoft entered the market late, but had the clout of a massive company behind it. In an effort to retain its market share, Netscape worked hard to improve its product. Microsoft then released a new version of their browser, and the browser wars quickly turned into a two-horse race. Because each company wanted to advance against the other, this category of software became quite sophisticated in a very short time, driving virtually all other competitors out of the market. Had either company established a clear lead, there would be little incentive for continuous improvement. With the Red Queen in action, customers now have access to far more sophisticated software that would be expected otherwise.

One of the challenges of working with biological metaphors is that most of us know less about biological systems than we do about Newtonian physics. There are lots of books on the topic you can read (including Kelly's book *Out of Control*), but for those of you who like to experiment with complex systems, there is some great software you can use.

If you are interested in exploring computer simulations of biological systems for which simple rules can lead to complex behavior (such as ant colonies and bird flocks), you might want to explore a programming language called *StarLogo*. This software can be found at http://www.media.mit.edu/ ~starlogo. If you've been involved with educational computing, you are probably familiar with the *Logo* programming language developed under the guidance of Professor Seymour Papert at MIT. This language allowed the creation of computer microworlds in which a virtual robot (called a turtle) can be programmed to move around the display screen in response to commands and procedures created by the user. Those of you who already know *Logo* will recognize much of *StarLogo*, but this new environment is not nearly as easy to master as the more-limited original versions of *Logo* — so be prepared to enter a steep learning curve.

StarLogo is a version of this language designed for the creation of microworlds in which huge numbers of turtles can be programmed to display certain behaviors based on their environment. By populating the microworld with large numbers of these turtles, each following simple rules, quite complex behaviors can result.

For example, a microworld based on ants might have the following rules for individual ants:

1. Move around the world randomly until you encounter food.
2. Pick up some food and start moving back to the nest.
3. As you move carrying food, leave a chemical marker that dissipates in a few minutes.
4. If an ant looking for food encounters a chemical marker trail, move toward the stronger end of the marker (*i.e.*, toward the food source).

The behavior of this microworld (populated with hundreds of ants) looks a lot like the behavior of real ants as they forage for food.

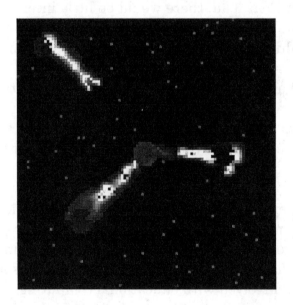

The small dots in the picture above represent ants. The diffuse light patches represent the chemical markers deposited by ants carrying food back to the nest in the center of the screen.

For a great introduction to *StarLogo*, you should check out Mitchell Resnick's book, *Turtles, Termites, and Traffic Jams: Explorations in Massively Parallel Microworlds.*

While *StarLogo* is a very powerful tool for exploring massively parallel microworlds, it does require some sophisticated programming skills to create these worlds in the first place. For example, the rule for getting the ants to move toward the food looks like this:

```
to look-for-food
if food > 0
   [setcarrying-food? true
    tsetfood food - 1
    setdrop-size 60
   rt 180 fd 1 stop]
ifelse chemical > 2
   [fd 1]
   [ifelse chemical < 0.05
       [wiggle fd 1]
       [uphill-chemical grid-step]]
end
```

I'm not saying that mastery of this language isn't worth the effort, just that *StarLogo* is not designed for casual users who want to experiment with model building.

A far more intuitive language for microworld creation is *Stagecast Creator*™, (based on the *Cocoa* technology developed at Apple Computer). *Stagecast Creator*™ is a programming environment in which the behavior of objects is determined by a series of rules (as in *StarLogo*) but in which the rules are created by physically demonstrating the behavior to the object itself.

You can explore the *Stagecast Creator*™ programming environment yourself by downloading a copy from http://www.stagecast.com. The best way to start with *Stagecast Creator*™ is to explore some sample microworlds that have already been created, and to look at the rules used to produce the behavior displayed by the various objects in the world. For example, a microworld based on a flower garden might include water that evaporates to form clouds, clouds that condense to produce rain, soil containing seeds to germinate, plants that grow or set blossoms when rained upon, blossoms that produce seeds when pollinated by bees, *etc.* Each object in this world has its own set of rules that governs its behavior. Once the microworld is started, the behavior of the entire system plays itself out on the screen.

59

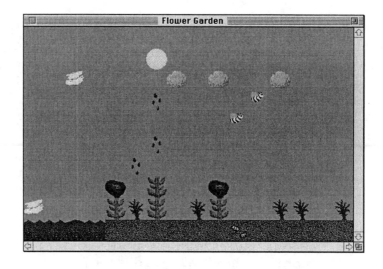

By examining a single object, you can see the rules it is programmed to follow. For example, here is a display of the rules relating to flower blossoms:

Errors in the behavior of an entire system can often be tracked to a particular object (or class of objects) whose rules can be adjusted to produce the desired results. *Stagecast Creator*™ is an ideal tool for exploring the dynamic biological metaphor in which complex behaviors can result from simple rules.

The central issue in any of the software tools we'll describe in the book is that the process of designing your model and testing it is far more important than the actual running of the final model. The end result (a working model) is a confirmation of your model building.

The process of designing a model will bring up all kinds of questions and force you to clarify your ideas in order to implement them in the microworld you are creating. I'll have much more to say on this topic in a later chapter, but I wanted to make this point here since it helps explain why *Stagecast Creator*™ may be a better tool for microworld creation than *StarLogo*. The process of creating and testing rules in *Stagecast Creator*™ is so simple, you never have to lose sight of the behavior you are trying to model.

Activities for this chapter:

1. How do you talk or think about your organization? What does your organizational chart look like? How is information shared within your organization? How are decisions made regarding customer service? The answers to these kinds of questions will tell you a lot about your organization, and its capacity to thrive in this world of rapid change.

2. What does your organization's chart look like? Is it hierarchical? Next, think about how work gets done in your organization — do you create informal teams across organizational boundaries? Does the "real" organizational chart reflect what is really going on? What steps do you think would lead to a more effective way of describing your organization?

3. Is your organization a candidate for networking? Look at your business or organizational procedures for opportunities to:

   - Distribute (Does everyone have to be in a central location?),
   - Decentralize (Are there opportunities for some of your organization's tasks to be outsourced?),
   - Collaborate (What natural strategic alliances can be formed with outsiders — even competitors?), and
   - Adapt (Is your organization flexible enough to respond quickly to new challenges?)

4. Download a copy of *StarLogo* from the MIT Web site (http://www.media.mit.edu/~starlogo) and run some of the examples. Read some of the documentation and look at the listings for some of the programs to see if you can figure out how they work. Change some of the properties of the behavior of the "turtles" and see how these small changes effect the behavior of the complete system.

5. Download a copy of *Stagecast Creator*™ from the Stagecast Web site (http://www.stagecast.com) and run some of the examples. Double-click your mouse on any object to look at its rules. After reading the tutorial documentation, create a simple microworld of your own based on a biological or business system. If you want to jump in and create a model of a real system, design a *Stagecast Creator*™ microworld with an intersection of two streets with gas stations at each of the four corners and create a model in which the popularity of a gas station is determined by price.

From Nouns
to Verbs

To keep up, you need the right answers.
To get ahead, you need the right questions.
— John Browning and Spencer Reiss

Earlier in this book I quoted the University of California, Berkeley professor, Ikujiro Nonaka who said, "The dynamics of knowledge have become the most important competitive resource of the firm." Notice that he is referring to the dynamics, not the knowledge itself — a reference to verbs, not nouns.

The idea that we live in a world where the process is at least as important as content is worthy of some thought. Obviously, you can't have pure process — actions must have things to act upon; yet the importance of the process is so great that it can determine the success of many ventures.

In education, there has been a move for some years toward a process-based curriculum — a curriculum based on thinking skills, information finding, writing process, creativity, and other verb-based activities. This move has come about partly in response to the realization that schools can never provide enough static facts to last a student for a lifetime, and the task of preparing students to become lifelong learners is critical to the success of the educational enterprise.

Many years ago, San Francisco longshoreman and philosopher Eric Hoffer said, "In a time of drastic change it is the learners who inherit the future. The learned usually find themselves equipped to live in a world that no longer exists." McDonald's founder, Ray Kroc, is reported to have expressed the idea this way: "When you're green you grow; when you're ripe, you rot." No matter how the idea is expressed, the message is clear — in times of great change, we all need to spend as much time working on the verb-aspects of our lives as we do on the nouns.

Central to this notion is the idea of lifelong learning. The rapid obsolescence of old information, coupled with the rapid pace of discovery, has created a world in which work and learning will be merging for many people.

Adaptivity, one of the characteristics of networked organizations we explored in the previous chapter, implies close attention to the verbs. One concept that applies in this view of the world is that of the "informated" object. Informated objects not only contain information, they facilitate transactions.

Take hotel keys, for example. Many hotels across the United States are using door locks that are opened with credit card-sized keys with a magnetic stripe on the back. Because these keys are programmed to be useful for a single stay, the hotel doesn't have to worry about lost keys. Typically, fresh keys are made when people check in. On the surface, the key contains information needed to verify that a certain door may be unlocked. In fact, these keys can be used to facilitate transactions as well. For example, some resort hotels pride themselves in having rooms made up while the occupants are at breakfast, or have left the room for some other activity. It is a simple matter for the master door lock computer to send a beeper message to housekeeping, letting them know which rooms were recently vacated and ready for cleaning.

Take this concept one step further. Checking into a hotel can take a long time when a lot of people arrive at the same time. For those customers who have already verified their reservation and are holding it with a credit card, a hotel could have an instant check-in location where the visitor could just insert the credit card for verification and have room keys issued automatically. This automated check-in would be a boon to the weary business traveler who just wants to get to the room as quickly as possible.

Another example of the shift from nouns to verbs is in the area of inventory control. Bar codes have been used for many years as a tool for labeling inventory. These passive messages have facilitated inventory management. But today a new technology is emerging with even more power: miniature transceivers containing a microprocessor and a two-way radio. These single-chip devices were pioneered by Micron Communications, and are about the size of a large postage stamp. In use, a special radio transmitter sends signals to a room full of packages who each send messages back about their contents.

One interesting application for this technology is in the area of automated gas pumps. A special key chain containing one of these devices can be detected by a gas pump as a customer pulls into the station. The customer can then simply pump gas right into the car and drive away, knowing that the key chain-based computer will have exchanged the relevant information with the computer at the gas pump. Similar technologies are showing up (in slightly larger form) at toll booths across the country, allowing people to drive through special areas where the computer chip in the car can send the authorizing message to the toll booth which will then receive the data and then update a monthly bill to the customer — all without requiring the driver to stop, fish for cash, and tie up traffic.

To see even more evidence of this shift from nouns to verbs, look at what has happened to personal computing in the past few years. A little over a decade ago most desktop computers operated in isolation. If they were connected to a network, it was primarily to connect to a printer. Today, networked computers are commonplace. As MIT's Professor Nicholas Negroponte says, "The future is in the network, not the node." It is the interconnection of our machines where the true power lies.

The most obvious manifestation of this is the incredible popularity of the Internet and the World-Wide-Web. The Network Computer (NC) is an extreme example of the shift from nouns to verbs. Generally, today, even networked computers contain a lot of applications and data. In the world of the NC, the computer on the desktop would contain some basic applications to communicate and display information retrieved from a remote server. No major applications or data would reside on the NC except when needed.

This aspect of network computing has some people to mistakenly think this is a return to the world of mainframes and dumb terminals. In fact, this is not the case. In the old terminal-based world, all the computation was done remotely, and the terminal served merely as a device for inputting and displaying information. A network computer is a very powerful device in its own right. In addition to the need to display and input information, the NC must also be able to run communications software and execute programs written in languages like Java. In this model, the role of the server is to hold the applications and data until they are needed. Once someone using an NC wants to run a word processor, for example, the word processing software is uploaded to the NC where it resides until the user wants to do something else. By "thinking globally and acting locally," the NC puts much less demand on the network and the central server than the old model of mainframes and dumb terminals.

The advantage of NC's for large organizations comes from the ease of upgrading software. When a new productivity tool is introduced, it can be installed on the central server, rather than requiring that each desktop computer be upgraded. Another benefit is that remote access to a corporate network can (in principle) be achieved through public access NC's located anywhere.

While many people use the Net for the exchange of information, it is increasingly finding use as a tool for collaboration. As videoconferencing moves to the desktop, the capacity for remote groups to collaborate on projects will increase tremendously. Nintendo has even released a digital camera module for its GameBoy product, suggesting that videoconferencing might even move to shirt-pocket-sized devices in the near future.

The challenge for collaboration is not technological. Desktop conferencing software has been available for free for several years (*e.g.*, Cornell University's CU-SeeMe software) and inexpensive color cameras for computers are commonplace today. The challenge comes from people who value their information, and want to hold onto it. Francis Bacon understood this power of knowledge when he said:

> **"Nothing destroys authority so much as the unequal and untimely interchange of power, pressed too far and relaxed too much."**
> **— Francis Bacon, 1601**

When we share knowledge with others, we share power as well. Many people think (as did Bacon) that it is a zero-sum game: for every winner there is a loser. Collaboration in the face of this mindset is virtually impossible. It is easy to get caught up on the nouns of our world — the things we know. Instead, we would do well to shift our focus to the processes by which we learn and apply new ideas — the verbs. Given the speed with which static ideas become obsolete, the desire to hang on to information seems strange, yet it is a common malady — a holdover from another time when the world was not in such a state of flux.

As I said before, it is not that the nouns of our world have lost their importance. There are lots of "things" that are of tremendous importance, and a core knowledge of these things is essential. By the same token, it is important to understand the underlying processes that act on the things around us, and to learn enough about these processes to use them to our own advantage.

The remainder of this book will focus on several processes of tremendous utility to everyone: educators, students, and business people alike. These are processes designed to help with thinking strategies. The development of thinking skills for a verb-based world, the world of chaotic time, is absolutely essential if we are to thrive in the coming years.

Activities for this chapter:

1. Think about your job. Is your value to your job derived from the information you have (the nouns), or from the processes you know (the verbs)? In all likelihood, you'll find it is a combination of both.

2. Using the form designed for this purpose at the end of this book, make a list of the major "nouns" of your profession (the bodies of factual information you rely on a daily basis) and, in the next column, make a list of the process skills you use in your job. Which column describes your greatest value to your organization? Do you think your answer would have been different if the question had been asked about your profession twenty years ago?

Language and Thought

The map is not the territory.
— *Anonymous*

The previous chapters have explored a future moving at light-speed. New paradigms of business and education are called for, and we've tried to illustrate some of these.

The deeper challenge is to identify the kinds of thinking skills that everyone can use to thrive in this topsy-turvy world — skills that can be applied on a daily basis to projects of all kinds. These skills make use of tools, some of which may be familiar to you, and some of which may not. This chapter is transitional. We will be leaving our description of the kinds of changes confronting organizations of all kinds, and focus instead on the kinds of thinking skills and tools that help us navigate the raging waters of the future with some sense of control.

If there is one skill that we can put at the top of our list, it is the capacity to think creatively: to be able to make meaning from incomplete fragments of information, to synthesize new ideas from existing parts, and, when no guidance is available, to chart a new course on our own. All the tools we'll explore in the following chapters are designed to assist in this process. If you're ready, you can leap ahead to the next chapter and get started. If you wish to skip this chapter altogether, you are free to do so. The only reason for sticking around is to get some background on a topic you might find interesting.

Let's start with an important idea: that the tools we use to represent information can influence the thoughts we think. We saw this in action in the chapter *From Focus to Peripheral Vision* when we talked about FAST diagrams. The process of taking verb-noun pairs and placing them in a hierarchy of abstraction helps identify the Highest Order Function of your enterprise. While you could have developed other ways to achieve this result, the spatial arrangement (and rearrangement) of functions helps focus your thoughts in productive ways.

Once again, when we explored traditional hierarchical organizational charts and network diagrams, we saw how the spatial representation of an organization could influence the way we thought about the group itself.

The human mind seems to work by associations, by building mental models; and the ways in which we think are controlled, in some sense, by the language in which we do our thinking. While the great architect, Louis Sullivan, believed that form follows function, it is probably more the case the function follows form, at least when we think about the impact of expressive modalities on thought.

Benjamin Whorf, a pioneer in the field of socio-linguistics, held that our thoughts are controlled by the language in which we think them. Whorf was careful to point out that thinking in language does not necessitate the use of words. He believed that much thinking involves the manipulation of paradigms — models of reality. If your paradigm reflects that of a linear hierarchical organizational structure, the creation of informal networks in your organization will be seen as chaotic and confusing. If, on the other hand, you think in terms of a chaotic model of time more adapted to the world of today, then networks make sense.

It is fascinating to me, for example, that chaos theory became popular as a field of scientific inquiry just as we started to experience the rapid acceleration of time we've talked about so far in this book. The seeds of chaos theory were sown many years ago, but prior to the invention of digital computers, this branch of science was considered intractable. While it is fascinating to see the language of chaos theory coming into existence just in time for its application outside its original domain, the more metaphysical among you might wonder if the emergence of this theory was just lucky happenstance.

In any event, we have always searched for models to explain what we see around us. We have always worked to develop expressive tools to facilitate our thinking processes. The tools we will describe in the following chapters are not particularly new, yet, like chaos theory, they have emerged just in time to play a powerful role in helping us develop and express ideas to assist in our management of life in this period of rapid change.

We'll be exploring, for example, the move from linear text to hypertext; from linear brainstorming to idea mapping, and so on. In each case we'll explore a familiar tool that still has great utility, but that, for certain applications, is inferior to newer tools available to us today. It is as if these new tools represent the new languages in which we can think the kinds of thoughts we need in order to thrive in today's world.

The culture of simulations

As we progress through the next few chapters, we'll explore several powerful tools, starting with expression, then creativity, then understanding, and, finally, tools for building models of complex systems. The field of complex systems is quite popular these days. One of the dominant business applications for computers is the spreadsheet program — basically a tool for building models.

While we'll explore other model building tools that are even more powerful than spreadsheets, it is important to distinguish between tools for simulation, and tools for model building. This is a topic close to the heart of Sherry Turkle, whose book, *Life on the Screen: Identity in the Age of the Internet*, has much to say on this topic. There is a lot of excellent software available for simulating all kinds of activities, from flying planes, to operating nuclear power plants. Even children have access to a rich array of simulation tools for exploring ecosystems, city planning, *etc.* As wonderful as these tools are, they suffer from a major flaw: the underlying assumptions of the simulation can not be modified by the user, and they are generally hidden from view. This leaves the user in the position of operating a simulation whose assumptions can't be challenged, or even made visible. While it might be argued that this is a case of art reflecting life, these programs rob the user of the chance to develop an important skill: that of model building.

When you construct a model yourself (of a business, or an academic topic) the very process of *designing* the model forces you to think deeply about the various factors that influence the microworld you are trying to create. You are forced to think about the interrelationships of the different parts of the model, and in the process, you develop a deep understanding of the system itself.

The actual implementation of your model as a working simulation is your reward. The real benefit comes from constructing the model in the first place. The kinds of thinking skills that are developed when you build models are different from those developed when you run simulations. It is the former area where the greatest payoff occurs.

71

When I express this idea in my seminars, I'm sometimes asked what happens when people create models using incorrect assumptions. The result, generally, is that the resulting model does not behave properly. The act of "debugging" the model to get the desired result provides a chance to further clarify thinking. Mistakes have their place in the learning process — they always have, and they always will. The beauty of model building is that you get to express and try out your ideas in a safe environment first, before letting them play out in the real world.

Some comments about computers

Because many of us take computers for granted, we don't often stop to think about the ramifications of these tools for expression. Most commonly, computers are used to create documents we previously made with other technologies such as typewriters. While this application has great utility, it hides the fact that fast modern personal computers allow the generation and expression of ideas that would be incredibly difficult or impossible to create any other way.

In an extraordinary article in the education journal, *Technos* (Spring, 1998), "The Leonardo Loop: Science Returns to Art," James Bailey provides compelling evidence that the rise of the mass-produced book tilted the expression of scientific ideas away from drawing and toward equations, not because equations were a better way to express ideas, but primarily because they could be set in type. Leonardo da Vinci is today acknowledged for his brilliance, yet he was criticized in years past because he never "published" his work. A quick glance at his notebooks reveals why: His use of words was strongly intermixed with drawings, and the printing technology of the day did not support the kinds of art Leonardo used to illustrate his ideas. With the rise of the mass-produced book in the 1500's, the world of holistic representation (pictures that can be understood at once) gave way to the linear sequential world of text. Bailey goes on to suggest that the very nature of scientific theory and inquiry was shaped by the limitations of print.

Fast-forward to today, where powerful laptop computers allow the creation of incredibly rich graphics with the capacity to build dynamic models (using tools like *Stagecast Creator*™, for example) that play out on the screen, and we see the opportunity for the tools of today to reshape the nature of inquiry and exploration.

In contrasting the world of pen and paper (art) with the traditional printing press (text) and today's computers (interactive models), Bailey draws the following conclusions:

The partnership of mind and pen has an emphasis on spatial relationships and on the art of seeing. Shapes are central.

The partnership of mind and book has an emphasis on linearity and the art of sequentializing. Symbols are central.

The partnership of mind and circuit (*e.g.*, networked computers) has an emphasis on adaptation and the art of recognizing. Patterns are central.

Our world today is one in which the last perspective is essential. The search for patterns in the midst of data overload is very important, and today's computers provide us with the capacity to conduct this search.

And so, with these thoughts in mind, let's move to the first of the shifts in expressive modalities that can have tremendous benefit in today's world: the expansion of linear text to hypertext.

From Linear Text to Hypertext

The human mind operates by association.
— *Vannevar Bush*

The development of print was one of the seminal inventions in the history of communication. The production of linear text in the form of mass-produced books, popularized by Aldus Manutius, took years to take the world by storm, but eventually this revolution reached virtually everywhere, and today we take books and other linear documents for granted.

There is little question that writing has tremendous value, and that the capacity to express ideas in written form is a mark of an educated person. Yet, in this time of rapid change, it is worth asking if the structure of traditional written documents is appropriate for all kinds of expression. This is especially important when the volume of text is growing at a prodigious rate. Scientific discoveries, new inventions, trade agreements, and a myriad of other developments seem to be coming at a faster and faster rate, and these documents are plugging up our capacity to make sense of them.

To say we live in a period of infoglut would be an understatement.

Is there a solution to the challenge of information overload? Can modern technologies provide us with other ways to publish and consult records of value to us?

These questions were asked by Vannevar Bush, science advisor to President Roosevelt. In an article, "As We May Think," published in the July 1945 issue of *Atlantic Monthly*, Dr. Bush suggested an alternative to the linear structure for representing textual information. The following passages from that article highlight the essence of his thoughts on the topic. As you read, remember that these thoughts were published in 1945.

The difficulty seems to be, not so much that we publish unduly in view of the extent and variety of present-day interests, but rather that publication has been extended far beyond our present ability to make real use of the record. The summation of human experience is being expanded at a prodigious rate, and the means we use for threading through the consequent maze to the momentarily important item is the same as was used in the days of square-rigged ships.

...

Our ineptitude in getting at the record is largely caused by the artificiality of systems of indexing. When data of any sort are placed in storage, they are filed alphabetically or numerically, and information is found (when it is) by tracing it down from subclass to subclass. It can be in only one place, unless duplicates are used; one has to have rules as to which path will locate it, and the rules are cumbersome. Having found one item, moreover, one has to emerge from the system and re-enter on a new path.

The human mind does not work that way. It operates by association. With one item in its grasp, it snaps instantly to the next that is suggested by the association of thoughts, in accordance with some intricate web of trails carried by the cells of the brain. It has other characteristics, of course; trails that are not frequently followed are prone to fade, items are not fully permanent, memory is transitory. Yet the speed of action, the intricacy of trails, the detail of mental pictures, is awe-inspiring beyond all else in nature.

...

Selection by association, rather than by indexing, may yet be mechanized. One cannot hope thus to equal the speed and flexibility with which the mind follows an associative trail, but it should be possible to beat the mind decisively in regard to the permanence and clarity of the items resurrected from storage.

Consider a future device for individual use, which is a sort of mechanized private file and library. It needs a name, and to coin one at random, "memex" will do. A memex is a device in which an individual stores all his books, records, and communications, and which is mechanized so that it may be consulted with exceeding speed and flexibility. It is an enlarged intimate supplement to his memory.

...

The owner of the memex, let us say, is interested in the origin and properties of the bow and arrow. Specifically he is studying why the short Turkish bow was apparently superior to the English long bow in the skirmishes of the Crusades. He has dozens of possibly pertinent books and articles in his memex. First he runs through an encyclopedia, finds an interesting but sketchy article, leaves it projected. Next, in a history, he finds another pertinent item, and ties the two together. Thus he goes, building a trail of many items. Occasionally he inserts a comment of his own, either linking it into the main trail or joining it by a side trail to a particular item. When it becomes evident that the elastic properties of available materials had a great deal to do with the bow, he branches off on a side trail which takes him through textbooks on elasticity and tables of physical constants. He inserts a page of longhand analysis of his own. Thus he builds a trail of his interest through the maze of materials available to him.

...

Wholly new forms of encyclopedias will appear, ready-made with a mesh of associative trails running through them, ready to be dropped into the memex and there amplified. The lawyer has at his touch the associated opinions and decisions of his whole experience, and of the experience of friends and authorities. The patent attorney has on call the millions of issued patents, with familiar trails to every point of his client's interest. The physician, puzzled by its patient's reactions, strikes the trail established in studying an earlier similar case, and runs rapidly through analogous case histories, with side references to the classics for the pertinent anatomy and histology. The chemist, struggling with the synthesis of an organic compound, has all the chemical literature before him in his laboratory, with trails following the analogies of compounds, and side trails to their physical and chemical behavior.

Does this all sound familiar? If you use the World-Wide-Web, it should. The connected associative trails that Bush describes today go by the name of hypertext, and Web pages are built from hypertext documents.

Notice that we have not discarded linear text, we have amplified it by building a process for establishing links between one part of a document and another, or between one part of a document and a different document located (today) nearly anywhere in the world.

It is fortuitous that the Web came into existence when it did. While hypertext tools existed prior to the Web, they required that all the linked documents reside in one location. The Web not only provides a hypertext medium, it creates the concept of documents extended globally, pieces of which are stored on computers in many countries.

Conduct a Web search on any topic, and you'll be directed to potentially relevant documents scattered all over the globe. This aspect of hypertext goes beyond Bush's vision, and it multiplies the power of his ideas.

This does not mean that the Web has solved our access problems, however. Like any expressive medium in its infancy, the Web is a pretty messy place. Many sites are littered with more buttons than a French accordion, and the elements of good page layout are often ignored. Even so, many people are finding the Web to be an indispensable tool in their day-to-day lives, especially for business and education.

In the beginning (1990) the Web was designed by Tim Berners-Lee at CERN (a Swiss research center) to be a pure hypertext medium through which research scientists could publish their work with embedded links to the work of their colleagues. Once the idea took off, the language of Web documents (HTML, or Hypertext Markup Language) was extended to allow graphics, sound, animation, and a host of other media types that now make the Web a multimedia haven.

If you are interested, there are lots of great books and software designed to ease your entry into the world of hypertext authoring. Many excellent authoring tools are available for free (such as *AOLPress* from http://www.aolpress.com). You should experiment with the creation of some hypertext documents yourself, even if you never post them to the Web, just to see if the capacity to link references or expand on an idea allows you to express ideas in productive new ways.

The key idea is that Web documents support associative links. As we mature in the use of this medium, its power to help us navigate and make meaning from huge amounts of information will only grow.

The problem with the Web...

While the dream of hypertext was that it would make it easier to locate and build associative trails through documents, many Web users feel more confused than ever. A search through a traditional library on some topic might produce a handful of references. The same search on the Web could produce thousands of relevant citations — far more than we are equipped to handle. This challenge will only increase as time goes on. A study conducted early in 1998 by the NEC Research Institute says the Internet has exploded to more than 320 million Web pages, an estimate that does not include millions of pages that are protected by passwords or "search walls" that block access to browsers or search engines. Add to this all the information available from other resources including on-line newsgroups and e-mail, then include magazine and journal articles and information you glean from internal memos, newspaper articles, and other sources, and you'll wonder how you will ever have the time to make sense of any of it.

One of the compelling challenges anyone in today's world faces is not how to access information, but how to find the specific pieces of information you need when you need them. As we mentioned before, context is king.

Finding contextual needles in informational haystacks is the job of "data mining," or "text mining" software. One of the pioneering projects in this arena took an interesting position: the best way to gather relevant information from very large text documents is to use pictures that represent maps of the document, rather than present the viewer with the text itself. The automated creation of contextual maps was pioneered by the Battelle Pacific Northwest National Laboratory (PNNL) under contract with the U.S. Department of Energy. PNNL was asked to design software that could help intelligence and national security research staffs efficiently access thousands of publications, documents, and transcripts strewn across the world.

The result was *SPIRE*, an acronym for "Spatial Paradigm for Information Retrieval and Exploration," a software system for transforming text-based information retrieval into a visual system for navigation, retrieval, and analysis. Over the last several years, *SPIRE* has been actively used by the U.S. intelligence community for research and analysis involving matters of national security.

ThemeMedia (http://www.thememedia.com) was created to commercialize this research effort, and is developing software tools for "content mapping" — a process that graphically represents thousands of unstructured documents pictorially on a single computer screen for quick, focused navigation, retrieval, and insight.

Today, the information search method of choice is based on Boolean logic, whereby a document must include one or more user-specified terms, or keywords, to make it eligible for consideration. Existing search engines, such as Excite, AltaVista, Lycos, and Infoseek (among others), typically generate a list of hundreds or thousands of documents, with only limited ability to order them by relevance. Furthermore, there is no common measure of relevance to help information seekers determine the true value of a document. Also, what AltaVista considers relevant for a particular query, Lycos may relegate to a position of less importance. Users are not only at the mercy of how each company defines relevance, they have no way of evaluating the methodology behind the retrieval process — no way of actually seeing the relationships among the documents listed.

The weakness of the Boolean search has to do with the user's role in two standard retrieval measures: precision and recall. Recall measures how well a search produces all the documents that fit the search criteria, while precision measures how successful the search is at eliminating irrelevant documents from that pool. If information seekers were capable of knowing exactly what they wanted and, then, how to ask for it, there wouldn't be a problem. But it's extremely difficult for most of us to state our precise information needs to a database we can't see and have never explored. As a result, Boolean searches often return too much irrelevant information or not enough of what we really need.

Visually-based software tools, like *SPIRE*, *SPIRIX* (being developed by ThemeMedia), and other excellent tools such as *VisualInsights* from Lucent (http://www.visualinsights.com), give users a quick way to actually see everything available to them from a given information set, with topics and documents grouped by degree of similarity and level of importance.

Generally, these programs analyze patterns of word usage and relationships between words, automatically discovering salient themes, deriving semantic distances between them to represent degrees of similarity, and transforming the results into visual representations arranged to reveal document relevance.

Tools like *SPIRIX* do not come cheap, however. Plan on spending a few thousand dollars for a copy that runs on your SGI workstation.

This does not mean that there are no good text mining tools for personal computers — there are, and they run on the inexpensive hardware we are likely to find in our homes, schools and offices. One excellent data mining tool is called *Xcize*, produced by Brosis (http://www.brosisii.com). This software builds indices of text documents and automatically builds correlation diagrams so that specific topics that appear in different documents can be isolated instantly. As with *SPIRE*, *Xcize* creates visual maps of a document. An *Xcize* map looks for matching patterns in text blocks, and plots colored dots on the screen to map the areas where areas of one document overlap with other areas of the same document, or where two documents appear to treat the same topic. A quick glance at this map identifies areas that can be profitably explored in further depth. As with *SPIRE*, *Xcize* can simplify the task of finding relevant information in large documents. The automated linkage of related words and phrases makes *Xcize* a hypertext tool in the sense that Vannevar Bush first envisioned it.

As the sheer volume of information continues to grow, data mining tools will increase in importance for business and educational audiences alike. The next few years will likely produce an explosion of such tools as we continue to find ways to make sense of a rapidly expanding universe of information. How fortunate we were that Bush had the insight to foresee a defining problem of our time, and to propose a solution that works.

Activities for this chapter:

1. Make a list of the kinds of Web sites you find most valuable in your day-to-day work. Make a list of their characteristics: are they updated daily (news sites)? Do they provide you with access to information you can't get in a timely fashion any other way? Do they provide useful links?

2. Download an HTML authoring tool (such as *AOLPress*) or get a copy of *PageMill* or *HomePage* and experiment with the creation of hypertext documents of your own. Do you see ways you could use hypertext to keep track of articles, research papers, business documents, etc?

3. If you are an educator or student, explore ways that hypertext documents could be used to build portfolios of your work. These portfolios could be posted on a school's server and shared with other teachers. Students could create hypertext documents that reference outside sources as well as the work of other students.

4. Explore data mining tools like *Xcize* (http://www.brosisii.com). Download the software and use it to help you extract valuable information from a large text document of your own.

From Brainstorming to Idea Mapping

The best way to predict the future is to invent it.
— *Alan Kay*

Any list of survival skills for today's fast-paced world would have to include creativity. The capacity to think creatively has always been needed, and that need is amplified today.

Many years ago, Alex Osborne (the "O" in the famous advertising firm of BBD&O) developed a process for generating and capturing ideas.

Rules for Brainstorming:

1. Start with a clear statement of the problem or challenge to be addressed — and be sure this problem statement is as broad as possible to encourage novel solutions.
2. Suspend judgment and watch for put-downs and other "killer" statements.
3. Have a facilitator create a list of every idea that is expressed by the group. When the flow of new ideas slows, keep the process going by injecting humor or some other method of changing people's frame of mind.
4. Write everything down, no matter how silly it sounds.
5. Encourage participation from everyone in the group.
6. Avoid detailed discussion.

The idea is to capture as many ideas as possible, no matter how irrelevant or silly some of them might seem, and then evaluate this list later. The suspension of judgment is critical to the process. You can't get hot and cold water out of the same pipe at the same time, so at the initial stage of the process make sure that no ideas are shot down.

Once a list has been created, then each item on the list can be evaluated, expanded upon, rejected, linked to other ideas, or form the basis for more brainstorming.

Ultimately, a set of viable ideas will emerge, often containing a few valuable nuggets that would never have surfaced otherwise.

To get a sense of the process, create a brainstorming session of your own (either by yourself, or with a group) around the following topic: You have just inherited a warehouse full of plastic drinking cups, but found that the traditional market for these cups has disappeared. Create a brainstorm on alternative uses for these items. (If you are working by yourself, stop after you have a list of 40 ideas).

How did you do?

If you are like most people doing this activity, you probably were able to get a dozen ideas out pretty quickly, but after awhile, you started to freeze up, and new ideas were hard to come by.

You might think this is because you are not a very creative person, but the problem is probably structural. Here's why.

When you are generating ideas, each new idea either represents flexibility or fluency. Flexibility refers to the generation of a completely new idea, for example:

> connect 2 cups with string to make a telephone system
> use cups to hold screws
> put straps on the bottom of the cups to make short stilts for house pets

Each of these ideas is distinct from the others, an example of flexibility.

Fluency refers to variations on a theme:

> use cups to hold screws
> use cups to hold nails
> use cups to hold paint

Each of these is a new idea, but they are all variations on a theme — the use of cups to hold something.

Fluency is great, as is flexibility. In fact, you should look at your brainstorming list to see how many examples of each you have. A good balance between the two is called for. As you scan your list, you may notice that examples of fluency are clustered together. Once you enter a theme (cups as vessels) you might stay with that application until you run out of ideas, and then move to a completely different application. The problem is, for many people, that it is easy to fall into a fluency trap — to keep developing variations on a theme until you get stuck, and then to have a hard time breaking free to generate a completely new idea.

Tony Buzan, Gabriele Rico, and others who have studied the creative process believe that the very structure of brainstorming can inhibit the generation of new ideas. Because a brainstorming session generates a linear text-based document, it can be hard to come up with a new idea.

The brain is very non-linear and has an incredible mass of interconnections in it. Buzan and Rico developed creativity tools that focus on the generation of maps — expressive representations of ideas that mirror, more closely, how our associative mind works. The general term I'll use to describe these representations is "idea mapping." An idea map is a highly interconnected document containing words and graphic linkages. The process of creating idea maps is quite easy to learn, and its application cuts across all creative endeavors. Buzan's work, for example, focused on the use of these maps for general creative problem solving, while Rico focused on mapping as a tool for writers. In fact, mapping is a great tool for just about anyone working on a project of any kind. This book, for example, was the result of an idea map on the topic of thinking skills for the 21st century.

One of the nice features of idea mapping is that it can function quite well both as a personal creative tool, and as a tool for small groups of people working together. Brainstorming, on the other hand, tends to work much better as a group-based tool than as a tool for individual creativity, primarily because of the danger of fluency traps. (I am indebted to Jim Fadiman for pointing out this limitation of personal brainstorming to me many years ago).

Let's start with a warm-up exercise (a worksheet for this exercise can be found in the *Activities* section at the back of this book).

Using this worksheet, or a sheet of paper on which you've drawn a central oval and ten ovals surrounding it, get prepared to write some words quickly. You'll start with a trigger word that I'll ask you to put in the center oval. As soon as you write this word down, your goal will be to write the next ten words that come to mind, one in each oval, writing as quickly as humanly possible. It is important that you do not think about the words you are writing and that you do not pause in the process. Just go with your stream of consciousness.

Before we start, I'll acknowledge that you might have a hard time doing this, but that's all right — just do the best you can, and keep repeating the exercise with trigger words of your own, until you can write ten words non-stop.

Ready? Here we go. Your trigger word is... TABLE

How'd you do?

Here is my map:

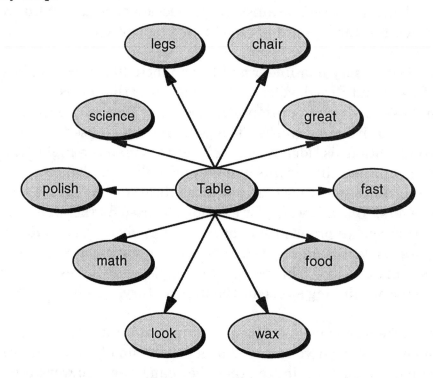

How many words do you have on your list that are also on mine? How many words do you have that have nothing whatever to do with tables? There are no right or wrong answers to this task. Just think of it as a game.

You'll probably find that you have a word or two in common with my list, but that the others will be wildly different. The point is that "free association" is not only free, it is unique. This uniqueness is exactly what idea mapping is designed to tap into. Your capacity to think wholly new thoughts can provide tremendous insights to any project you are working on. It doesn't matter if you're a student working on ideas for a term paper, or an entrepreneur thinking about starting a new business. The capacity to tap into your creative resources is of tremendous value.

Now for the creation of an idea map. The rules are pretty simple:

Rules for Idea Mapping:

1. Write a word and/or draw a picture that represents the central idea of the topic on which you wish to create your map. This should be in the center of a sheet of paper — perhaps a very large sheet of paper (such as butcher paper that can be purchased at most warehouse clubs these days). The advantage of using words *and* pictures is that each of these expressive modes can trigger thoughts from different parts of the brain. Years ago we used to associate words with the left hemisphere and pictures with the right hemisphere of the brain. No matter where these expressions call home, you'll want to use *all* of your brain, so think about words and pictures that will instantly trigger your mind to think about the subject of your idea mapping task.

2. Once you've got your central idea in place, draw a line and write the first word that comes to mind. Pay no attention to whether this word relates to your idea or not. If it pops into your mind, write it down.

3. If the word you just wrote triggers another word, then draw a line from the one you just wrote and place it there.

4. Keep going until you run out of ideas and feel yourself starting to slow down.

5. When you get stuck, or slow down, go back to the center, look at the central idea, draw a new line from it, and repeat the process described above.

6. Under NO circumstance judge any of the ideas you have written down. At this point you don't care about relevance, spelling, penmanship, drawing ability, or anything — all you are doing is capturing ideas. The time for editing comes later.

7. Once you have worked on your map for awhile (say 15 to 30 minutes — probably less at first), stop to look at your map and see what other connections make sense to you. Draw links between words or ideas from different parts of the map that may be related to each other. This is also a good time to make note of relevant ideas you might wish to explore further.

8. It isn't uncommon to find that some of the peripheral ideas relate quite strongly to your central problem, perhaps providing a better definition for the task at hand. If this is the case, then create a new idea map on a fresh sheet of paper with this new idea as the central theme.

The following is the start of a map I created on the topic of what it will mean to be an educated person in the 21st century:

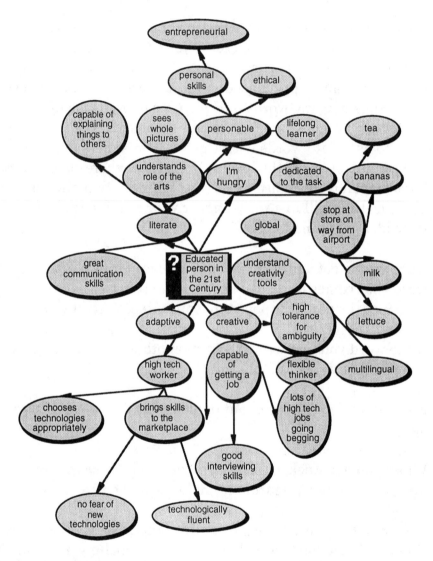

Once you've completed your map, you'll have a lot of ideas written down, and some of them probably have nothing whatever to do with your task. For example, I created the map above on a flight home from Chicago, and suddenly realized that I needed to stop at the store on my way home. The beauty of idea mapping is that, if the thought pops into your head, you just write it down — whether it seems relevant or not.

The reason for this is pretty simple. If you *don't* write down something you are thinking about, you're likely to get stuck on that thought and not be able to get back to your project. So, if you think it, write it down — you can always discard ideas later.

Idea maps can quickly grow quite large. The following map (reduced to fit on the page) represents about 15 minutes of work around a topic of relevance to one of my commercial clients:

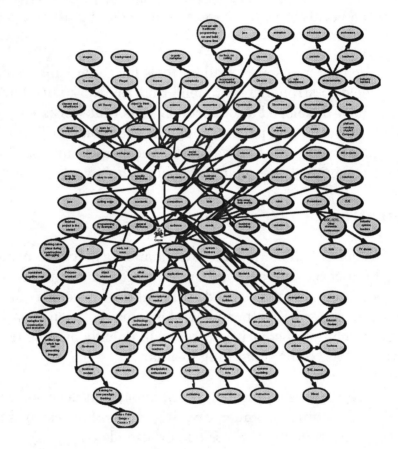

What on Earth do you do with a mess like this?

That brings us to the next stage of idea mapping — the refinement of your ideas into some useful form. At this point you are less interested in generating new ideas (although that is almost always welcomed), and you are more interested in looking for those ideas that provide insights to your central question. One way to accomplish this task is to use a colored marker to highlight the ideas that strike you as particularly relevant. Once you've done this, you can start incorporating these ideas into a report or a plan for a project.

The "right" way to create maps...

There *is* no one right way to create a map. Each individual develops his or her own personal mapping style, and this is the right approach to take. As David Hyerle says in his book, *Visual Tools for Constructing Knowledge*:

> Brainstorming webs should be honored as "sacred" in the sense that the free associations and links among ideas are more like an evolving piece of art than a document to be evaluated using comparative methods. Within this framework of respect for individual thinking, there is no "wrong" use of webbing, only more productive techniques that students can learn for improving their abilities to tap the flow of their creative juices.

Hand-made idea maps are excellent tools for generating and capturing creative ideas. I strongly recommend that you work with hand-drawn maps until you have developed a comfortable style that works for you. One limitation of pencil and paper, though, is that you'll still have to transcribe your results if you want to use them in another document. Fortunately, there are some computer-based mapping tools to help you.

Inspiration

There is a special challenge that idea mapping software needs to address: it must get out of the user's way. In other words, the software for capturing ideas needs to work at the speed of thought — to work as fast as ideas can be scribbled on paper with a pencil. Unless this criterion is satisfied, anyone engaged in a burst of creative process will quickly become frustrated, and have the process come screeching to a halt.

Fortunately, there is a program, *Inspiration*, that does a superb job at capturing ideas quickly while providing some other features to simplify the future organization and expression of these ideas.

Inspiration (available for both Mac and Windows) not only lets you create idea maps quickly, it produces very legible results, and allows the information you collect to be exported as a picture file of the map, or as text. *Inspiration* was used to create the maps and some other drawings in this book.

One of the most useful features of *Inspiration* is its "RapidFire" mode. When this option is chosen, you just click your mouse inside an oval representing an idea that is triggering your thoughts, and start pumping out related ideas as fast as you can, pressing the "Return" key after each one. As time permits, *Inspiration* will sort out these ideas into ovals of their own, all automatically linked to the seed idea. You don't have to hunt for a fresh location on the screen to add a new idea — the program finds one on its own. If you decide to print a copy of your map, the program can automatically redraw a large map to insure that text does not overlap a boundary between pages (making the assembly of a large map quite easy). *Inspiration* has many other features that make it worth exploring, so you should download a demonstration copy from their Web site (http://www.inspiration.com) and try it yourself.

Activities for this chapter:

1. Using the template in the activities section of this book, create a brainstorm on alternative uses for plastic drinking cups. When you are done, analyze your list for examples of flexibility (completely new ideas) and fluency (variations on a theme). If you got stuck during the process, look to see if you were caught in a fluency trap.

2. Using the same template as the previous exercise, create a brainstorm on the topic of what it will mean to be an educated person in the 21st century. Compare your results with the list you generated in the chapter entitled, *The Future Isn't What it Used to Be.*

3. Do a rapid idea mapping warm-up using the appropriate form at the end of this book. Set a stopwatch (or look at a second hand on a clock) and, when you start, write the word "table" in the central oval and, as quickly as possible, write the next ten words that come to mind in the spaces around this central oval. The goal here is speed, not relevance. Repeat this activity on a regular basis (using a different word in the center of the diagram) until your capacity to write words is limited by your handwriting speed.

4. Using the form at the end of the book, create an idea map on this topic: What will it mean to be an educated person in the 21st century? Remember to start by placing the central idea in the middle of the chart and to keep the process going as long as possible. Compare your idea map on this topic with the brainstorm list you did in activity 2. Did you generate new ideas using idea mapping? Which approach worked best for you? Which produced the greatest number of ideas? Which approach produced the best ideas?

5. Download a demo version of *Inspiration* and explore the features of this software as a tool for generating idea maps. Compare the use of this software with your experience of making hand-drawn maps. What are the benefits and limitations of each approach? What features would you incorporate in your "ideal" idea mapping software?

From Outlines to Concept Maps

Where is the knowledge we've lost in information?
— T. S. Eliot

Just about everyone is taught how to create outlines in school. The need for an outline prior to writing a paper is accepted without question in many quarters, even though many people find it easier to generate an outline *after* they have written their paper.

Outlines are built around the hierarchical sequencing and nesting of information. The task of creating an outline involves moving in two directions at once — first, through the large scale organization of a linear document, and, second, through the detailed development of each major section. The resulting structure is shown visually:

I.
  A.
     1.
        a.
        b.
     2.
        a.
  B.
     1.
II.
  A.

and so on.

To set the stage for the rest of this chapter, you should create a small outline of your own on some topic of interest to you. I'd suggest doing one on the role of technology as a learning tool, since this probably is a topic close to your heart.

How did you do? Did the outline flow easily, or did you find yourself bouncing back and forth between the big picture headings and the nested levels inside each one? Did a concept deep in the hierarchy suddenly trigger a new major topic heading for you — requiring you to restructure your outline?

Outlines are easy to read, but not always easy to create. One of their challenges is not just that they represent information hierarchically, but that this information is represented by a "tree," rather than as a "network." Trees have branches with unique connections to nodes where they connect to larger branches, and so on, until they join the main trunk. Networks have branches as well, but these branches can have multiple connections — they can represent information more naturally, in some cases, than trees.

As with brainstorming, the linear nature of outlined text can sometimes inhibit the process of expressing ideas and relationships. One solution to this dilemma is called "concept mapping," developed by J. D. Novak and D. B. Gowin (as described in their book *Learning How to Learn*).

Concept mapping is a tool that allows you to build a representation of your understanding of a concept. Unlike idea mapping, which is designed to support the capture of creative brainstorming sessions, concept mapping is designed to let you find and express relationships between various concepts you have written down. Where idea maps are free-form, concept maps are hierarchical, building from the general to the concrete as you move down the hierarchy. Idea maps often work with nouns; concept maps have nouns (concepts) in boxes, and the links between these boxes are labeled with verbs describing the relationship between the words in the boxes at either end of a link. Concept map links can be uni- or bi-directional, and there are as many variations of concept mapping as there are for idea mapping.

One powerful use for concept mapping in education is to get a picture of a student's current understanding of a topic before it is taught. Then, after a subject has been explored, the student creates a new concept map. By comparing the two maps, students can see what they have learned — what misconceptions they may have had, and what breadth and depth has been added to their understanding.

This is not to suggest that concept mapping is used purely in an educational setting — it has tremendous application in business as well, for everything

94

from exploring organizational structures to developing strategies for new product development.

Now for the creation of a concept map. The rules are pretty simple:

Rules for Concept Mapping:

1. Take a project or topic you want to explore and make a list of all the concepts you can think of that relate to this topic. These will most likely be nouns.

2. Put these concepts in boxes arranged under the main topic in such a way that related concepts are near each other (just to keep your map from getting too cluttered).

3. Build links between related concepts and label the links with descriptive verbs that describe the connections you are making.

4. If you wish, you can clarify your map by having it move hierarchically from the most general to the most specific concepts as you move down the page. When you are done, your concept map should be easy for you or someone else to read.

One way to facilitate the concept mapping process is to write concept words on individual cards or PostIt™ notes so they can be easily arranged on a sheet of paper before building the links.

Concept maps can be of any size — ranging from a handful to many hundreds of concepts. The following figure shows a small (and highly incomplete) map I created on the uses of technology in learning.

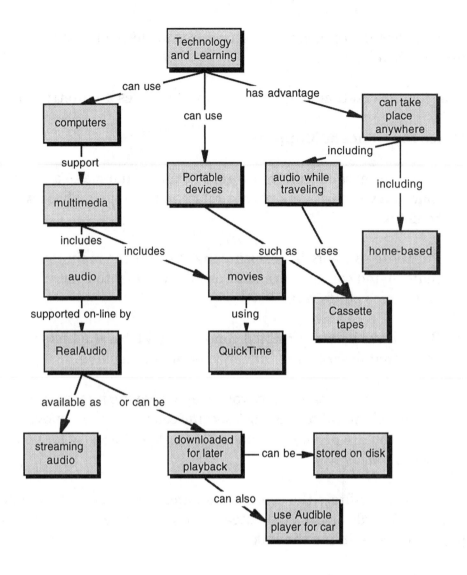

Now that you see what a concept map looks like, it is time for you to build one of your own. So you can compare your results with the outlining task, create a concept map on the topic of technology as a learning tool. (My map is highly incomplete — feel free to make yours as large as you wish!) Start by making a list of relevant concepts, and then build the linkages between them. Be sure to label your links with verbs that describe the connection between the linked concepts.

You may find that you've included concepts that have no obvious linkages. In this case, ask yourself if the concepts relate to the topic, or if they need some bridging concepts that you have to learn about before completing your map. The nice thing about concept mapping is that it can sometimes help you identify questions that need to be answered before you can complete your task.

How did you do? You probably were able to express a lot of concepts quickly, (especially if you used idea mapping as a tool for generating concepts), and you were probably able to build linkages that made sense without too much trouble.

As you gain more experience with concept mapping, you'll find that a completed map can make a great presentation handout when you are sharing some new ideas with an audience. If you do this, be sure to encourage others to add to or modify your map as they build connections of their own.

Inspiration

In addition to being an excellent tool for idea mapping, *Inspiration* can also be used to build concept maps. Text can be added to links just as easily as it can to boxes, and Inspiration incorporates a layout tool that draws hierarchical maps that are easy to read. Because the goal of concept mapping is to construct an easy-to-read document that flows nicely from the general to the specific, tools like *Inspiration* are of great value — especially if you are building large concept maps.

CMap

Years ago (around 1990) Scott Hunter and Howard Stahl created a concept mapping tool for the Macintosh called *CMap*. While *CMap* is not elegant, it is a very compact and fast tool for creating concept maps. It lacks the nice formatting features of *Inspiration*, but still contains the basic abilities to create concepts and links. Completed maps can be pasted into any application. You can download a copy from http://www2.ucsc.edu/mlrg/mlrgtools.html

The following figure shows a small concept map created in *CMap*.

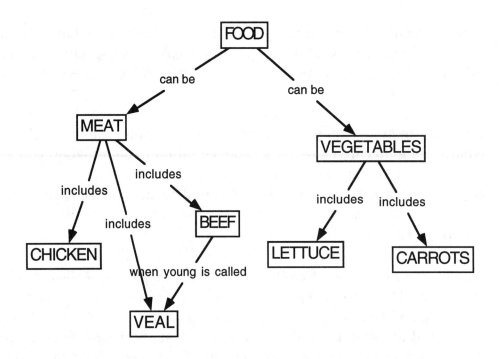

LifeMap

Another concept mapping tool worth exploring is called *LifeMap*, created by Dr. Robert Abrams. This Mac-based program contains many features, including a "rapid-fire" mode for capturing concepts, similar to Inspiration. Because *LifeMap* was created specifically for concept mapping as an educational tool, its examples are related to academic projects. The completed maps lack the formatting features of *Inspiration*, but *LifeMap* has many features that make it worth looking at. The latest version can be downloaded from http://www2.ucsc.edu/mlrg/mlrgtools.html

Model-It

While the previous three software tools are designed to create easy-to-read concept maps, the final product is (usually) a static printed document. Imagine, though, a concept mapping tool that has two additional features: it can include quantitative relationships in its links, and the resulting map can be "run" as a computer program so these relationships can be explored in a dynamic fashion.

This is the task of an excellent program, *Model-It*, created by Prof. Elliot Soloway and his team at the University of Michigan for both the Mac and Windows platforms (http://www.cogitomedia.com).

Model-It allows you to create "objects," each of which can have "factors" or measurable aspects of these objects. For example, you might create an object called "Ocean" that has factors like "Depth," "Salinity," "Available light," "Temperature" — in short, anything you can measure in an ocean. Once you have defined some objects and their factors, you can build relational links between the factors of one object, or between factors of the different objects in your model.

Unlike traditional concept maps in which these links are just verbs, the links in *Model-It* are relationships that can be expressed in semi-quantitative or quantitative fashion. For example, suppose you have created an "Ocean" object with the factors "Depth" and "Available light." As each factor is created you are given the opportunity to specify a minimum, maximum and starting value for the factor. For example, "Depth" might start with zero and range from zero to 4,000 meters — the choice is up to you. If you build a link between "Ocean Depth" and "Ocean Available light," for example, you will be given the chance to define a relationship between these two factors as shown in the figure below:

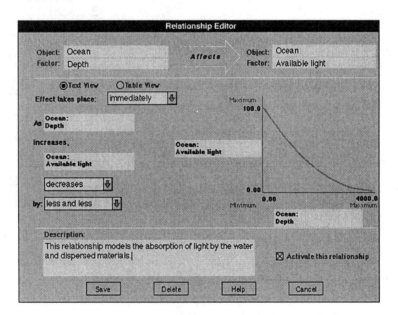

In this case, I have chosen to have the available light decrease as depth increases, and have even specified that the light decreases by "less and less," reflective of an exponential drop-off in available light as depth increases. The process of thinking about the detailed relationship between two factors in your model is tremendously important, since you are forced to examine your understanding of these relationships in order to build them. In traditional concept mapping you might indicate that light decreased with depth, but this observation does not specify *how* the relationship between depth and available light looks.

Once you have built the relationship links, you can attach meters and slide controls so that, when you run the model, you can control depth, for example, and see how the available light changes as a result of your virtual dive into the ocean.

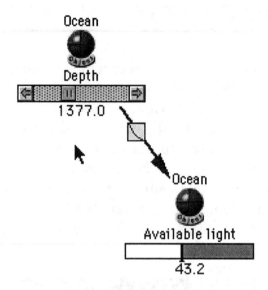

Model-It allows various factors to be plotted on a graph as the model is run. The insights generated as a result of building, testing, and refining your model can be incredibly useful.

For example, you could build a model of a business in which customers are sensitive to price, and find an optimal price point for your product by building a simulation of customer behavior. As you experiment with Model-It, you'll find yourself thinking carefully about the systems you explore with it.

Activities for this chapter:

1. Using the template in the activities section of this book, create an outline on the topic of technology as a learning tool. Notice your process. Did the topics and subheadings flow easily? Did you find yourself changing topic levels as you thought about your outline? Did a concept at a deep level of the outline trigger new ideas for higher-level concepts?

2. Using the template in the activities section of this book, create a concept map on the topic of technology as a learning tool. Remember to start by making a list of all the concepts you can think of related to this topic. Place these concepts in boxes. Next, connect the boxes with links containing verbs describing the connection between two concepts. Compare this experience with the outline you created in the first activity. Which tool was easier? Which produced richer results? Which provided the best way for you to build a hierarchical structure for your ideas?

3. Download copies of *CMap* and *LifeMap* from http://www2.ucsc.edu/mlrg/ mlrgtools.html and use them, along with *Inspiration*, to create some concept maps on your own. Which computer-based tool do you like best? Why? What features would you include in your ideal concept mapping software?

4. Download a copy of *Model-It* from http://www.cogitomedia.com and use it to create a concept map in which you include some qualitative modeling. What kinds of applications can you envision for this tool? Can you apply it to some aspects of your business or profession? If so, build an interactive dynamic concept map and see what insights you can glean from running your model.

From Spreadsheets
to Causal Loops

Where is the wisdom we've lost in knowledge?
— *T. S. Eliot*

As powerful as concept mapping is, it suffers from a limitation common to many representational structures — it is hierarchical and the flow of a process is generally one-way. At first glance, this might not seem to be a limitation, but it is. It is easy for us to think in a linear hierarchical way, since it mirrors our most common use of language. The noun-verb-noun structure of simple sentences leads to the ready representation of thought in the form of *a* causes *b*. This linearity of cause and effect is implicit in many tools we've explored so far — including concept mapping. It also forms the foundation for many of our analytical tools, including spreadsheets.

Spreadsheets are one of the three or four top business applications for computers today. While spreadsheet software is a powerful tool for displaying and manipulating data, it has its downside: it promotes "spreadsheet thinking." Spreadsheet thinking has two aspects to it — first, the implication that all important information can be represented numerically; and, more insidiously, that the chain of cause and effect is linear.

To see a situation where spreadsheet software is *not* appropriate, suppose you have a product for which the demand is increasing. In an attempt to keep maximize your revenues, you raise your price. This, however, reduces demand, causing you to lower your price again. The resulting surge in demand entices you to raise your price again. If you were to build a spreadsheet model of this process, you would be tempted to express demand as a function of price, and price as a function of demand. As soon as you do that on any spreadsheet program I've encountered, you get an error message like this:

 Can't resolve circular references.

The problem with spreadsheets is that they can't handle feedback loops. They are designed to function in a world of unidirectional cause and effect. While there are many applications for which spreadsheets make sense, they are tremendously limited by their inability to model complex systems containing one or more feedback loops. There are other tools better suited to this task (as we'll see later), but first we need to explore the reason for learning about them.

The need for systems thinking

Consider the following scenario: you run a company manufacturing high-tech gadgets and you notice that your sales for the previous month took a precipitous drop. What do you do?

The rational first step is to look for an immediate solution to this problem — offer a special promotion, or step up an ad campaign, for example. In other words, your logical first step is to respond to the *event*. If you do this, and your sales bounce back, you might think the problem is solved and go no further — until disaster strikes again.

A better choice would be to look at historical sets of sales data for your product to see if you can uncover any underlying *patterns* in your sales — patterns that pointed to the possibility of a sales dip, for example. Once you've done this you are getting closer to identifying the root of your problem, and are thus closer to finding a deeper long-term solution.

But there is one more step that is of great importance, the task of identifying the underlying *structure* of the system that produces the pattern you've observed. By understanding the factors that comprise your entire system (in this case, including manufacturing, distribution, marketing, sales, R&D, *etc.*) you'll be able to peer into the future to see what effect various changes in one part of the system (*e.g.*, increasing R&D) might have on product sales.

Systems thinking is involved with the analysis of the underlying structure of a dynamic process, and it is a skill of tremendous value, since it is the best way to develop insights with some measure of long-term value. In their book,

104

Systems Thinking Basics: From Concepts to Causal Loops, authors Virginia Anderson and Lauren Johnson distinguish between events, patterns, and structures this way:

	Way of perceiving	Action	Time
Events	Witness event	React!	Present
Patterns	Track patterns	Adapt!	↓
Structures	Systems thinking	Change!	Future

While reacting to events and adapting to patterns is important, real change is facilitated by a deep understanding of the system that produces the patterns and events you have observed.

What is a system?

As stated by Anderson and Johnson in their book, a system has five qualities to it:

1. A system's parts must all be present for the system to carry out its purpose optimally.

2. A system's parts must be arranged in a specific way for the system to carry out its purpose.

3. Systems have specific purposes within larger systems.

4. Systems maintain their stability through fluctuations and adjustments.

5. Systems have feedback.

Using these criteria, let's explore some candidates to see if they are systems. Remember that systems must have all five parts present.

Is a basket of candy a system? How about a child going out for "trick or treat" on Halloween?

Let's start with the basket of candy. In this case we have a collection, not a system. Here's why. First, all the parts do not have to be present. You can take a piece of candy, and still have a (slightly smaller) basket of candy left. Second, the candy can be piled in the basket in any order. While it is possible that the basket of candy might have a specific purpose within a larger system, it is not a system itself. And, any fluctuations and adjustments are made externally. A basket of candy lacks feedback.

Now, let's look at a child going out "trick or treating." In this case:

1. The child has to be costumed, have a basket for candy, a flashlight if it is dark, and it must be Halloween.

2. The costume must be worn, not carried around in a paper sack.

3. The costume and candy-hunting routine fits in with the larger system of Halloween tradition and depends on the systems of the candy givers, the candy manufacturers, and others to work properly.

4. The goal of a full basket may determine how many houses are visited based on the amount of candy received at each house.

5. Feedback on costume and conversation takes the form of compliments and the amount of candy given.

Because each of the five rules works for this example, we can safely call it a system. Why is this important? Because systems are commonplace in our world, and if we are to influence them, we first need to be able to identify them. Our bodies contain several systems (digestive, circulatory, *etc.*) Our institutions (schools, businesses) comprise systems, although man-made systems are rarely as complex as natural systems.

To hone your capacity to identify systems, try the exercise on this topic listed in the *Activities* section. After a little practice, you'll develop a good sense of what does, and what does not, constitute a system.

When you understand the underlying structure of a system that is responsible for some behavior that has caught your attention, your capacity to shape the future course of this system (or at least understand it) has increased immeasurably. "Causal loops" are diagrams you can create to serve as powerful tools for representing the underlying structure of a system. The process of defining these loops requires that you explore the five elements of your system described above. The process of analyzing your system so you can generate a causal loop diagram often provides tremendous insights as to why a system behaves the way it does, and points out those aspects of the system that you might want to change in order to optimize the behavior of the system as a whole.

The major advantage of systems thinking is that it gives you access to the "big picture." Consider the following case study:

XYZ Corp. has recently found its help desk swamped with calls from customers who are having a hard time understanding how to use some of the features of their products.

The *event* is a sharp increase in help-line requests, and the corporate response to this event is to add more phone lines and personnel to handle the calls.

A more productive approach might be to look at historical data on requests for help to see if there is an underlying *pattern* that emerges over time, and if this pattern is related to other events taking place in the company. Basically, the goal is to look at the behavior of different aspects of the company over time to see what emerges. One way to perform this task is to sketch a simple graph of the various events over time, to see if they appear to be related. For example, the following simple graph shows how help requests, new product introductions and sales changed over time.

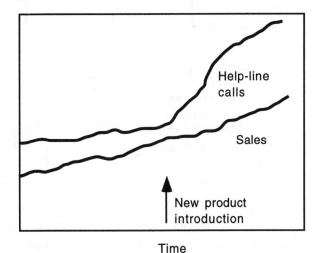

Time

This graph reveals some useful information that is absent when you just look at the event itself: help-line calls started after the introduction of a new product. This suggests that we broaden our view to see if there are ways of addressing the problem on a structural level, rather than just responding to the event itself by adding more capacity to handle the calls. For example, what does the introduction of a new product have to do with the increase in help requests? Is it the case that the new product has some flaws, or that it needs better documentation? We wouldn't have known to look at these issues if we hadn't explored the behavior of the system over time.

The next step in system analysis is to build a model of the underlying structure of the process to see if we can replicate the behavior represented in the graph. The tool we'll use for this is a "causal loop" diagram. A causal loop is a pictorial representation of a feedback loop in which a change in one parameter changes the next one in the loop, which changes the next, and so on until the last item in the loop changes the first item.

For example, let's build a loop based on the original event: after the introduction of a new product, calls to the help line increase, overwhelming the help desk. The overwhelmed help desk needs assistance, increasing the hiring of new help personnel. The increased hiring allows the increased number of calls to be handled effectively (at least until another new product is introduced).

A causal loop for this process might look like this:

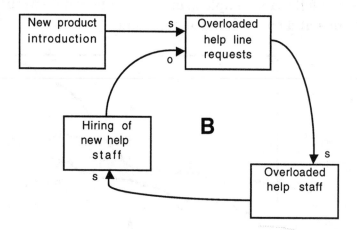

There are a few things to notice about this diagram. First, note that each arrow has either an "s" or an "o" next to it. This indicates the direction of change in the effect. Because an increase in help-line overload causes an increase in the same direction in the overload experienced by the staff, we have an "s" at the arrow. Because hiring new staff reduces the overload on the help lines, a move in the opposite direction, we put an "o" at the end of that line. The overall effect of this loop is to balance out the overload (by hiring more staff). As a result, this is called a "balancing" loop, and that is why it has a "B" in its center.

Causal loops are of two types: balancing and reinforcing. A reinforcing loop keeps making a variable larger and larger (or smaller and smaller) over time. These loops would have an "R" in the middle. It is easy to see if a causal loop is reinforcing or balancing: reinforcing loops have all "s" or "o" arrows (or an even number of each), and a balancing loop has a mix of "s" and "o" arrows, but an odd number of each.

For more information on building causal loops, you should read the book by Anderson and Johnson mentioned above, or check out Peter Senge's book, *The Fifth Discipline*.

Try your hand at building a causal loop diagram of your own. In this case, use the help desk example again, but create a loop indicating what would happen if the product documentation were improved. In this case, you will have to add a delay, since there would be a time lag between when the product manuals were changed and when these manuals made their way into the hands of customers.

Delays are important, since they can have profound impact on the behavior of a system. In our fast-paced world of instant gratification, it is easy to react to an event in a way that produces short-term benefits, but long-term disaster. For example, imagine a company whose profitability was increased by laying off workers — including closing the R&D department. Over the short term, profits might go up as sales of existing products continued with reduced personnel costs. Eventually, the absence of new product updates would cause sales to decline, and without a new product development team, the company would go bankrupt. Companies that run themselves off of spreadsheets might never see this disaster coming. This is a prime example of why systems thinking is such an important skill.

By the way, if you think this example is far-fetched, I can give you quite a few case studies where this is *exactly* what some companies did just a year or two before they went out of business. A causal loop diagram showing this process has two loops in it: a balancing loop in which layoffs increase profitability, and a reinforcing loop (with a delay) in which profitability declines over time until the company collapses. If the impact were immediate, no one would take this risky course, but because there are short-term gains, event-driven decision makers can fall into a trap from which they'll never escape.

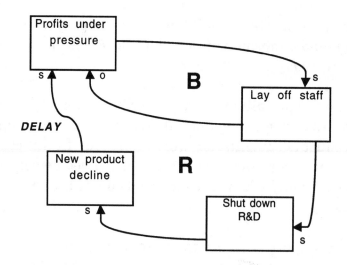

While tremendous insights can be gained by building hand-drawn causal loop diagrams, computer-based tools allow you to test your models to see if they show the behavior you are observing in the actual system They also allow you to create "what if?" scenarios of systemic changes you might want to make, with the advantage of trying them out on the computer before testing them in the real world.

Unlike spreadsheets designed to create tables of numbers, systems modeling software let's you build complex simulations of actual processes, complete with feedback loops.

Stella (also known as iThink)

This product was probably the first commercial software ever created for systems modeling, and it has been undergoing refinement for well over a decade. *Stella* is the flagship product of High Performance Systems, and a demonstration version can be downloaded for free from their Web site: http://www.hps.com

Stella is the optimal tool for building quantitative causal loops of any complexity. The system model is represented visually, and an individual element of the model can hold numbers or relationships between other parts of the model to which it is connected. For example, the following figure shows a simple reinforcing loop built in *Stella*:

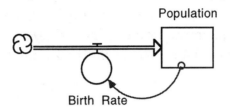

Population

Birth Rate

In this figure, the rectangle is a reservoir — a place where things (in this case, population) are accumulated. The "pipe" connecting this reservoir has a valve that lets new population enter the reservoir. This valve (called Birth Rate) in this example, is controlled by the current population through a relationship I created when I built the model. The relationship I created was that the birth rate at each instant of time was one-tenth the current population. This mathematically defined a reinforcing loop leading to an exponential rate of growth. (The cloud to the left of the pipe indicates an infinite reservoir of source material — whatever is appropriate for the model being created).

Once a model is created (and this is about the simplest model there is), you can create a graph to plot several variables over time.

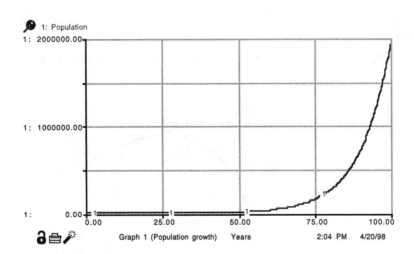

This population graph, for example, shows the exponential growth curve expected for our model.

The ability to have *Stella* generate graphs is one of its most important features, since you can compare these graphs with the ones you made prior to designing your model to see if you have correctly simulated the observed behavior of your system.

Models with several interacting loops are easy to construct with *Stella*. The following figure shows a simple predator/prey model that produces an oscillating result: as the Lynx population increases, the Hares are killed in greater number, reducing their supply, causing the Lynx population to decline. Once the Lynx population declines, the Hares have fewer predators, and their population increases. The cycle then repeats itself.

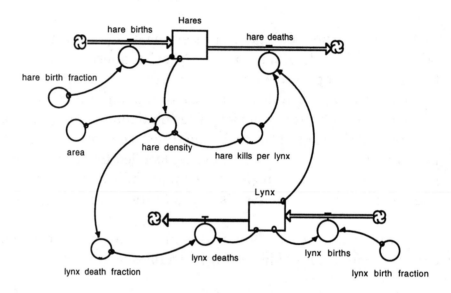

Another nice feature of *Stella* is its ability to automatically build a causal loop representing your model. This provides you with another way to see if your Stella model represents the process you are trying to model.

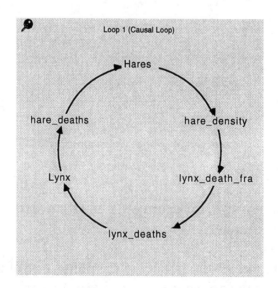

Because systems thinking is so strange to those of us brought up in a world where linear cause and effect were taught as the norm, it takes a lot of time to master this skill. Of the thinking skills I've explored in this book, this one is, by far, the most difficult. It is also one of the most powerful, because it is one skill that has predictive power.

Even if you never get to the stage of creating causal loops as easily as you'd like, you'll find yourself thinking in new ways. You'll find yourself looking for the "big picture" when you encounter a challenge in your organization. You'll find yourself looking for patterns, and for the underlying feedback loops that might be responsible for the patterns you observe.

Fortunately, systems thinking has become a popular topic in the past few years, so there are lots of resources available to help you gain mastery of this topic on your own. My goal in this chapter was to establish the need for this skill, and to illustrate some of its basic properties. The rest is in your hands.

Activities for this chapter:

1. To hone your capacity to identify systems, try the exercise on this topic listed in the *Activities* section. After a little practice, you'll develop a good sense of what does, and what does not, constitute a system.

2. Try your hand at building a causal loop diagram of your own. Use the help desk example again, but create a loop indicating what would happen if the product documentation were improved, thus reducing the need for adding long-term additional help-line staff. In this case, you will have to add a delay, since there will be a time lag between when the product manuals are changed and these manuals make their way into the hands of customers. You might want to create a more complex diagram using two coupled loops — one for the short-term fix (adding staff) and one for the longer-term solution. A form for this task can be found in the *Activities* section of this book.

3. Using the form in the *Activities* section at the end of this book, examine a recent event that had an impact on your business or organization.

    A. What was the event, and how did you react to it?
    B. Create a graph of the processes your organization was going through over time as it related to the event, with special focus on things that were going on prior to the event itself.
    C. Based on insights you may have obtained from this process analysis, create a causal loop diagram describing the processes you observed, or new processes you might implement to resolve the issue over the long-term.

Some Closing Thoughts

If you keep doing what you're doing, you'll keep getting what you've got.
— *Anonymous*

The twentieth century is drawing to a close. You can be sure the next two or three years will be filled with forecasts, guesses and wild hunches as to what the new millennium will bring. If the history of forecasting is our guide, most of these projections will be wrong.

If that is the case, then what about this book? What if I am wrong?

I have avoided trying to forecast the future. Everything I've written about in the opening chapters has already happened. As amazing as some of these things are, I expect the future to be loaded with even more amazing things — things we can't imagine today. And, so I will make a prediction. My prediction is that the future will be unpredictable. I predict that this period of rapid change in which we find ourselves will continue. I predict that the growth of new information will continue, and that our need to make meaning from this deluge will not decrease. I believe that the inversion processes that have moved us from diminishing returns to increasing returns, for example, will continue to reveal themselves in many new areas.

And, even if I am wrong, the skills we've explored in this book still have great utility. By focusing on skills rather than events (hence the subtitle of this book, *Thinking Skills for the 21st Century*), no matter what details the future has in store for us, tools for thinking will be of great utility. These skills would be useful even if the world were *not* changing in the ways I've described. None of the tools I mentioned is particularly new, yet few of them are in widespread use.

I was just thinking about the quote attributed to the great thinker, Abraham Maslow, who said, "If the only tool you have is a hammer, you tend to view all problems as if they were nails." Most of us developed facility with linear text-based tools, appropriate for many, but not all, tasks. For this reason, I chose to emphasize non-linear image-based tools since, if nothing else, they help round out the collection in our toolbox.

I hope this journey has been useful to you. I hope you have done the exercises in this book and have uncovered at least one tool, strategy, or way of thinking about the world you can apply on a regular basis. If so, then you will have been justified in reading this book, and I will have been justified in writing it.

Thanks for letting me share these ideas with you.

Activities

The activity sheets on the following pages are for your use in doing the various exercises in this book. You may, if you wish, make copies for your personal use. If you wish to use these activities with groups, please contact the author first.

Thinking About the Future: In the space below, make a list of what it will mean to be an educated person in the 21st century.

Linear and Chaotic Time: In the columns under each picture, make a list of practices in your organization that are reflective of the linear model of time, and then list alternative practices that reflect the chaotic model of time.

Linear model of time

Chaotic model of time

Butterflies and Strange Attractors: In the columns under each picture, make examples of "butterfly effects" and "strange attractors" relevant to your organization or field of expertise.

Butterfly Effects

Strange Attractors

_____   _____

_____   _____

_____   _____

_____   _____

_____   _____

_____   _____

_____   _____

_____   _____

_____   _____

FAST Diagramming: Create a Function Analysis System Technique diagram to identify the highest order function of your organization or profession. First create a list of verb-noun pairs that describe various functions of your activity. Next, arrange them in sequence in order of decreasing abstraction from left to right. When you are done, enter the verb-noun pairs in the boxes below. If you've done the task properly, each box to the left answers "Why?" and each box to the right answers "How?" The left-most box represents the highest-order function of your enterprise. (Note we have stacked continued lines of boxes vertically to fit them on the page).

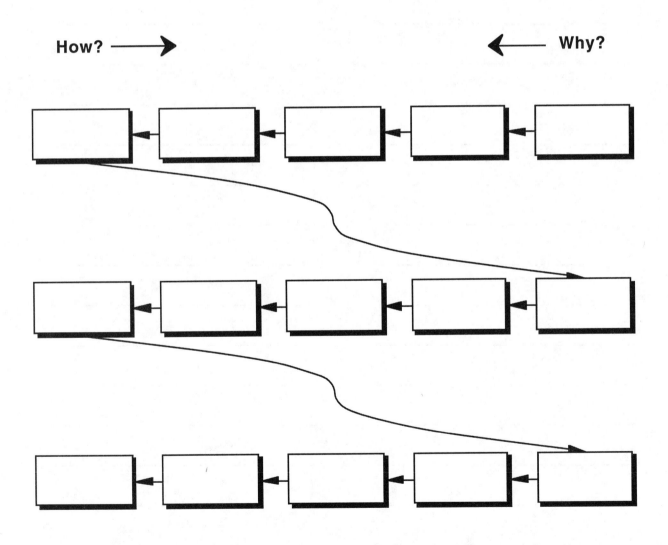

Verbs and Nouns: Make a list of the major "nouns" of your profession (the bodies of factual information you rely on a daily basis) and, in the next column, make a list of the process skills you use in your job. Which column describes your greatest value to your organization? Do you think your answer would have been different if the question had been asked about your profession twenty years ago?

Nouns (the stuff you know)   Verbs (the processes you know)

_____   _____

_____   _____

_____   _____

_____   _____

_____   _____

_____   _____

_____   _____

_____   _____

_____   _____

_____   _____

_____   _____

_____   _____

_____   _____

Brainstorming: In the space below, quickly make a list of 40 uses for a plastic cup.

_____   _____

_____   _____

_____   _____

_____   _____

_____   _____

_____   _____

_____   _____

_____   _____

_____   _____

_____   _____

_____   _____

_____   _____

_____   _____

_____   _____

Warming Up: Idea mapping warm-up — write the word "Table" in the central oval, then write the next ten words that pop into your mind in the surrounding ovals. Do this as quickly as possible.

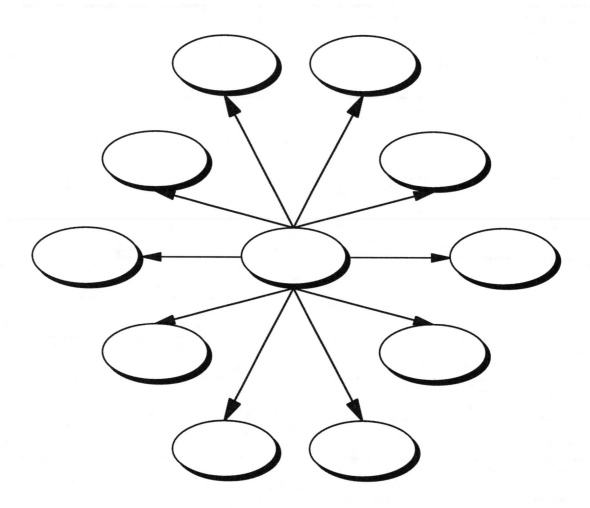

Idea Mapping: Create an idea map on a current professional or personal project of yours. (Remember to write or draw a picture reminiscent of the central idea of your project in the oval first).

Idea Mapping: Create an idea map with your ideas on what it will mean to be an educated person in the 21st century.

What will it mean to be an educated person in the 21st century?

Outlining: Create an outline for a report on some area or topic in which you have some expertise.

I.
   A.
      1.
         a.

II.
   A.
      1.
         a.

III.
   A.
      1.
         a.

Concept Mapping: Create a concept map for some area or topic in which you have some expertise. (Remember that nouns go in boxes or ovals, and verbs go on the lines connecting these nouns).

Identifying systems: All systems have these five components:

1. A system's parts must all be present for the system to carry out its purpose optimally.
2. A system's parts must be arranged in a specific way for the system to carry out its purpose.
3. Systems have specific purposes within larger systems.
4. Systems maintain their stability through fluctuations and adjustments.
5. Systems have feedback.

Using these criteria, determine which of the following are "systems," and explain why or why not.

A. A heater with a thermostat in a house
B. A refrigerator
C. A third-grade class
D. Your car
E. The task of painting a house
F. The creation of a new company
G. Growing a rose garden
H. Driving to work
I. Windows '95
J. Being in love

Causal loops: A company has introduced a new product, and the number of calls to the help-lines is rising quickly. Create a causal loop indicating what would happen if the product documentation was improved, thus reducing the need for adding long-term additional help-line staff. In this case, you will have to add a delay, since there will be a time lag between when the product manuals are changed and these manuals make their way into the hands of customers. You might want to create a more complex diagram using two coupled loops — one for the short-term fix (adding additional help staff) and one for the longer-term solution.

Causal Loops: examine a recent event that had an impact on your business or organization.

A.   What was the event, and how did you react to it?
B.   Create a graph of the processes your organization was going through over time as it related to the event, with special focus on things that were going on prior to the event itself.
C.   Based on insights you may have obtained from this process analysis, create a causal loop diagram describing the processes you observed, or new processes you might implement to resolve the issue over the long-term.

Software

Most the following software is available both for the Apple Macintosh and Windows '95 as well. Some titles are for only one platform (Macintosh, Windows '95, or Silicon Graphics UNIX) at the time this book was written. Demo versions of most of the titles could be downloaded for free from the listed Web sites.

AOLPress   (http://www.aolpress.com)
CMap   (http://www2.ucsc.edu/mlrg/mlrgtools.html)
Stagecast Creator™   (http://www.stagecast.com)
Inspiration   (http://www.inspiration.com)
LifeMap   (http://www2.ucsc.edu/mlrg/mlrgtools.html)
Model-It   (http://www.cogitomedia.com)
SPIRIX   (http://www.thememedia.com)
StarLogo   (http://www.media.mit.edu/~starlogo)
Stella   (http://www.hps.com)
VisualInsights   (http://www.visualinsights.com)
Xcize   (http://www.brosisii.com)

Bibliography

Anderson, Virginia, and Johnson, Lauren, *Systems Thinking Basics: From Concepts to Causal Loops*, Cambridge, MA, Pegasus Communications, 1997.

Arthur, W. Brian, "Increasing Returns and the Two Worlds of Business," *Harvard Business Review*, (July/August (1996): 100-109)

Bailey, James, "The Leonardo Loop: Science Returns to Art," *Technos* (Spring, 1998).

Bush, Vannevar, "As We May Think," *The Atlantic Monthly*, July, 1945.

Buzan, Tony, *Use Both Sides of Your Brain*, New York, Dutton, 1976.

Cerf, Christopher, and Navasky, Victor, *The Experts Speak: The Definitive Compendium of Authoritative Misinformation*, New York, Pantheon Books, 1984.

Christensen, Clayton M., *The Innovator's Dilemma: When New Technologies Cause Great Firms to Fail*, Boston, Harvard Business School Press, 1997.

Davis, Stan, and Meyer, Christopher, *Blur: The Speed of Change in the Connected Economy*, Reading, Addison-Wesley, 1998.

Gleick, James, *Chaos — Making a New Science*, New York, Viking, 1987.

Hyerle, David, *Visual Tools for Constructing Knowledge*, Alexandria, VA, ASCD, 1996.

Kelly, Kevin, *Out of Control: The New Biology of Machines, Social Systems, and the Economic World*, Reading, MA, Addison-Wesley, 1994.

McKenna, Regis, *Real Time: Preparing for the Age of the Never Satisfied Customer*, Boston, Harvard Business School Press, 1997.

Novak, J. D., and Gowin, D. B., *Learning How to Learn*, New York, Cambridge University Press, 1984.

Osborne, Alex F., *Applied Imagination: Principles and Procedures of Creative Problem-Solving*, New York, Scribner, 1963.

Peters, Thomas J., and Waterman, Robert H. Jr., *In Search of Excellence: Lessons from America's Best-Run Companies*, New York, Warner Books, 1982.

Peters, Thomas, *Thriving on Chaos: Handbook for a Management Revolution*, New York, Alfred Knopf, 1988.

Resnick, Mitchell, *Turtles, Termites, and Traffic Jams: Explorations in Massively Parallel Microworlds*, Cambridge, MA, MIT Press, 1997.

Rico, Gabriele L., *Writing the Natural Way: Using Right-Brain Techniques to Release Your Expressive Powers*, Los Angeles, J. P. Tarcher, 1983.

Senge, Peter M., *The Fifth Discipline: The Art & Practice of The Learning Organization*, New York, Doubleday, 1990.

Turkle, Sherry, *Life on the Screen: Identity in the Age of the Internet*, New York, Touchstone, 1995.

Wheatley, Margaret J., *Leadership and the New Science: Learning about Organization from an Orderly Universe*, San Francisco, Berrett-Koehler, 1994.

Whorf, Benjamin, Carroll, John B., ed., *Language, Thought and Reality; Selected Writings*, Cambridge, MIT Press, 1956.